COUNTRY
COOKING
from a
Redneck
KITCHEN

COUNTRY COOKING

from a

Redneck

KITCHEN

FRANCINE BRYSON

with ANN VOLKWEIN

CLARKSON POTTER/PUBLISHERS

NEW YORK

Copyright © 2016 by
Francine Bryson
Photographs copyright ©
2016 by Sara Remington

Published in the United States by
Clarkson Potter/Publishers, an imprint
of the Crown Publishing Group, a division
of Penguin Random House LLC, New York.
www.crownpublishing.com
www.clarksonpotter.com

CLARKSON POTTER is a trademark and
POTTER with colophon is a registered
trademark of Penguin Random House LLC.

Library of Congress Cataloging-in-
Publication Data
Bryson, Francine.
    Country cooking from a redneck
kitchen / Francine Bryson with
Ann Volkwein. — First edition.
        pages   cm
    Includes index.
1. Cooking, American—Southern style.
I. Volkwein, Ann. II. Title.
    TX715.2.S68B7954 2016
    641.5975—dc23
2015017785

ISBN 978-0-553-44845-0
eBook ISBN 978-0-553-45914-2

Printed in China

Book design by Sonia Persad
Cover design by Laura Palese
Cover photography by Sara Remington

10 9 8 7 6 5 4 3 2 1

First Edition

For my husband, Mark,
and my daughter, Sarablake,

for always being there, supporting and pushing me,
to live my lifelong dream;
for being my favorite recipe testers;
and for taking the dog out at 4 a.m. every day so I can sleep.

Contents

Introduction

Once your lifelong dream has been fulfilled, what do you do next? That's the question that kept running through my mind after I wrote my first cookbook, *Blue Ribbon Baking from a Redneck Kitchen*. After a whirlwind book tour, I suddenly had a bestseller on my hands. Then I got the call that gave me the answer. My editor asked, "Are you ready to write another cookbook?" Of course! So here we are, doing it all again, lifelong dream round two, and I couldn't be more grateful.

Many of you know that I am a proud national pie champion who cherishes every blue (and pink and red . . .) ribbon I have ever won. But most people don't know that my first foray into the cooking competition circuit, at age sixteen, featured a savory dish—an apricot-stuffed pork loin—that won first place in its category (see page 74). After that I was hooked and started experimenting with all of the classic Southern recipes I had grown up with. I tweaked and tinkered until I had something that tasted even better than the original—or until I proved that the original was, indeed, the best recipe ever.

While my friends wanted to be doctors and lawyers when they grew up, I hoped to become Julia Child or June Cleaver. My life revolves around food and always has. I come from a long line of Irish people who hold family in the highest regard. And if you really want to show someone you love them, there's no better way to do so than by cooking for them. That's what I learned from the women in my family. My nana (Mama's mom) put the bee in my cooking bonnet. She taught me how to make my first pie crust at the age of four and let me climb up on a chair in her kitchen to stir the green beans for Sunday dinner. My granny (Daddy's mom) was the mac-and-cheese maker. We had a standing date every Saturday. We would ride the bus into downtown Greenville and head to Tanner's Big Orange for orange juice and a chaser of little gold-wrapped coffee candies. Back in the 1970s, before malls and superstores, downtown was the place to be for the best restaurants, bakeries, and shops. Granny would tell me stories of where I came from, how life during the Depression was, and how I am so much like my daddy that I should have been a boy. This all happened over food.

My mother and grandmothers never had a stand mixer between them, but that didn't stop them from baking and cooking up a storm. We thickened our casseroles the old-fashioned way: by cooking butter and flour together to make a roux. While the term "roux" may sound fancy, a roux couldn't be simpler to make. I watched those ladies stretch a dollar "'til it squeaked," as my mama said, and make something from nothing. I was also taught how to use canned goods that were on sale to make a dinner that didn't taste like it came from a can, and to whip up meals using the staples in our pantry between grocery store visits. Whenever we could, we grew our own food because we had the space in the yard and the vegetables we harvested were plentiful and cheap. Cooking what's local and in season has become a trendy thing, but every redneck knows it's the cheapest way to feed your family well! When you stop to think about it, hunting and fishing are organic minus the packing house and all the fancy labels.

The recipes in this book are the ones that we Southerners go to when company shows up, when there's a dinner on the ground, or when the preacher is coming to visit. I was taught how to make great food that sticks with you and meals that get you through a day of hard work. It's not the fancy stuff served up with three sprigs of whatnot and a spoon of sauce artfully drawn on a plate, all to make you forget the food ain't that good—or plentiful. No, the recipes in this book are Southern through and through, the ones people have been asking me for years to share. You'll find Daddy's church chili (see page 112), the Roberts family's best fried chicken (see page 34), the meatloaf Nana taught me to cook so I would be a proper housewife (and believe me my husband is thankful she did; see page 83), and the holiday dressing I have spent years perfecting (see page 40)—to the point that it is requested at every family function, no matter the time of year. Of course, I'm also offering up some of my very best baked goods, including an upside-down apple bacon pie (yes, you read that right; see page 206) that is sure to make you the talk of the town—in a good way.

I want to make you the hero of your kitchen, serving Southern food with pride. I hope that this book makes y'all as happy as my first book did and that you can turn to it even more often—not just when you want something sweet. So gather your family around the table, have everyone check their screens at the screen door, and get ready for lots of full-belly good-food moans, smiles, and compliments.

Coconut Party Dip,
page 13

REDNECK WHATNOTS

Dips, salads, and finger foods that everyone will love

One of the phrases we love most here in the South is: "Company's coming," which is always followed up with: "Cha eat yet?" Feeding people is what we do, forever offering up something to munch on. We love to be social and so we don't hesitate to drop in on one another. Sometimes you have a warning, sometimes you don't. . . . If you aren't serving a whole meal, you're going to at least make sure guests leave with something in their bellies. That's what this chapter is all about—being prepared with that little something to serve.

COCONUT PARTY DIP

CHILI CHEESE DIP

Garden Dip

DEVILED HAM DIP

MOST-REQUESTED SPINACH DIP

Watergate Salad: Nana's Must-Have

PICNIC TABLE CUCUMBER SALAD

AUNT FANNY'S BUTTERMILK SALAD

Old-Fashioned Squash Relish

CORNBREAD SALAD

GRITS AND BACON FRITTERS

Green 'Mater Chow Chow

Coconut PARTY DIP

Mama used to make this dip—even when it was cold outside. It's always made me feel like I was sitting out on a deck with waves splashing, a breeze in the air, and palm trees rustling. She served it with fruit or crackers as a simple treat or for entertaining. I think it makes a sweet and creamy starter for a tropical theme party or picnic.

MAKES ABOUT 5 CUPS

```
4 ounces cream cheese, at room temperature
1 (7-ounce) jar marshmallow creme (I like Fluff)
1 (3.4-ounce) box coconut instant pudding mix
1 (8-ounce) can crushed pineapple
1 (8-ounce) container frozen whipped topping, thawed
1 cup sweetened coconut flakes, toasted
Fruit, graham crackers, vanilla wafers, and/or pretzel sticks,
for serving
```

1. In a stand mixer fitted with the whisk attachment, whip the cream cheese until smooth. Add the marshmallow creme and pudding mix and whip until the mixture is light and fluffy and the pudding mix dissolves and is no longer gritty, about 3 minutes.

2. Drain the crushed pineapple in a fine-mesh sieve. Don't hesitate to use your hands to squeeze down on the pineapple until most of the juice is drained off. Add the crushed pineapple to the cream cheese mixture and whisk until just combined. Fold in the whipped topping.

3. Transfer the mixture to an airtight container and refrigerate until well chilled, at least 1 hour and up to 3 days.

4. Top with the toasted coconut and serve with fruit, graham crackers, vanilla wafers, and/or pretzel sticks, for dipping.

Chili CHEESE DIP

Now who doesn't love chili and cheese on cold days? This one is meaty, loaded with gooey cheese, and guaranteed to warm you right up. I like to serve it on game day with those sturdy little bowl-shaped tortilla chips for easy scooping.

MAKES ABOUT 4 CUPS

1 pound 90% lean ground beef
8 ounces cream cheese, at room temperature
2 cups shredded cheddar cheese
1 (8-ounce) can RO*TEL diced tomatoes (you can use the ones with chiles, for extra bite)
1 habanero pepper, seeded and finely diced
1 tablespoon sugar
2 tablespoons chili powder
Hot sauce (I use Texas Pete)
Tortilla chips, for serving

1. In a deep skillet over medium-high heat, cook the ground beef, breaking it up with a spoon, until browned and cooked through, about 10 minutes.

2. Drain the fat off and then return the pan to the stove over low heat. Add the cream cheese, cheddar cheese, tomatoes, habanero, sugar, chili powder, and hot sauce to taste. Stir until well blended.

3. Serve warm with tortilla chips.

Garden DIP

This creamy vegetable dip has a ranch dressing flavor but isn't quite so ranch-y (is that a word?). When I was pregnant with my daughter, ranch dressing was my number one craving and I just could not get enough. This recipe was a good choice for satisfying that craving and is nice whenever you need a little taste of something much better than any of the premade dips found at the store.

MAKES ABOUT 3 CUPS

1 cup sour cream
½ cup mayonnaise (I use Duke's)
½ cup finely diced red bell pepper
½ cup finely diced yellow bell pepper
¼ cup finely diced green onions
¼ cup chopped radishes
1½ tablespoons sugar
1 teaspoon Worcestershire sauce
Salt and black pepper
Carrot and celery sticks, or chips, for serving

1. In a medium bowl, mix together the sour cream, mayonnaise, bell peppers, green onions, radishes, sugar, and Worcestershire sauce; season with salt and pepper. Cover and refrigerate for at least 1 hour and up to 3 days to allow the flavors to mingle.

2. Serve with carrots and celery or your chip of choice.

Deviled HAM DIP

I don't know where deviled ham came from, or where eating something called deviled became acceptable, but boy do we love it! Mama used to have this dip made up at all times in case the preacher might drop by (which is pretty funny, when you think about it) or for when I had friends over. It's still one of the things I make on a moment's notice to serve when company shows up. It's meaty and smooth, with bold flavor and a good bite at the end because of the horseradish.

MAKES ABOUT 2 CUPS

½ pound thinly sliced deli ham, chopped
8 ounces cream cheese, at room temperature
2 tablespoons mayonnaise (I use Duke's)
1½ tablespoons prepared horseradish
1 tablespoon grated onion
1 teaspoon garlic powder
Pinch of black pepper
Toasted bread or crackers, for serving

1. In a blender, combine the ham, cream cheese, mayonnaise, horseradish, onion, garlic powder, and pepper and blend until smooth. Transfer to an airtight container and refrigerate until well chilled, at least 1 hour or up to 3 days.

2. Serve this spread on little pieces of toasted bread or buttery crackers.

Most-Requested SPINACH DIP

I have an awesome girlfriend named Charlie who loves this flavorful spinach dip more than life itself. In fact, she and my husband, Mark, share that opinion, so this recipe is a must at every function we share as a group. There's something addictive about the light texture combined with the rich and earthy big flavor. Mark has gone so far as to hide the dip and to growl at anyone who finds it and takes a bite. As a result, I often double this recipe, to make sure we have enough to go around, and serve it in a scooped-out bread bowl.

MAKES ABOUT 3 CUPS

1 (12-ounce) box frozen chopped spinach
12 ounces sour cream
½ cup mayonnaise (I use Duke's)
1 tablespoon Montreal steak seasoning
2½ tablespoons dried onion
1 (0.9-ounce) package Knorr Spring Vegetable Recipe Mix
(it has to be Knorr)
¼ teaspoon salt
¼ teaspoon sugar
Wheat Thins, for serving

1. Put the spinach in a microwavable bowl and microwave for 3 minutes. Stir and then cook for an additional 2 minutes. Transfer to a strainer to cool and then use your hands to make sure all the water is squeezed out.

2. In a medium bowl, mix together the sour cream and mayonnaise. Add the steak seasoning, dried onion, vegetable mix, salt, and sugar and stir until well blended. Stir in the spinach and let sit in the refrigerator for at least 1 hour and up to overnight for the flavors to develop.

3. Serve with Wheat Thins for dipping.

Watergate Salad:
NANA'S MUST-HAVE

Christmas, Easter, Thanksgiving, dinner on the ground—you name it: This sweet "salad" made its way to the table. One taste and I'm a kid again, one of the ones who gets fed first! There are some things made with instant pudding that just don't taste right if you make them from scratch, and this is one of them. I just can't get enough of this sweet and creamy pistachio and pineapple appetizer. I'm not sure where this recipe came from—I've read that it's from the Watergate Hotel in Washington, D.C. All I know is that it's become a family favorite; I still make it just like Nana (and so many others) did.

SERVES 10

1 (18-ounce) can crushed pineapple
1 (3.4-ounce) box pistachio instant pudding mix
1 (8-ounce) container frozen whipped topping
(or more to taste), thawed
3 cups mini marshmallows
1 (8-ounce) jar maraschino cherries, drained

1. Pour the pineapple and its juices into a medium bowl. Add the pudding mix and mix well. Stir in the whipped topping and marshmallows. Garnish with cherries.

2. Chill for at least 2 hours before serving (I let mine sit overnight).

Picnic Table CUCUMBER SALAD

Picture this: It's summertime, it's hot, and you have a whole plate of ribs on the picnic table. This cool, tangy salad is the perfect thing to go with those hot sticky ribs. It makes a great snack or side, and it's just plain good.

SERVES 4

3 medium cucumbers, peeled and chopped
2 large beefsteak tomatoes, diced
1 medium red onion, diced
¾ cup distilled white vinegar
½ cup sugar

Put the vegetables in a bowl and stir in 1 cup cold water, the vinegar, and sugar. (I put it all in a big canning jar and shake well.) Let sit in the refrigerator for at least 30 minutes and up to 3 days before serving. The longer it sits, the better it gets.

TO BE A BLUE RIBBON WINNER

1. Don't stress yourself out.
I had to learn that the hard way. I would be so nervous about a contest that I wouldn't be able to eat or sleep for days before.

2. Practice, practice, practice.
Feed your trial efforts to people you know well, or even people at work, but make sure you're feeding people who will give you an honest opinion, not ones who will say it's good even if they hate it. I always turned to my dad before he passed last year. Now my husband and my best girlfriends are my guinea pigs.

3. Think outside the box.
If you are inspired to put something together and you think it will make people smile, then go for it. If it seems strange in the common world but you think it is a good mix, most of the time others will, too.

4. Presentation is key.
Give your entry a cute name—if the name is catchy, most of the time the judges will like what you made even before tasting it. Make sure your entry looks good, as people eat with their eyes first. Always go for the extra flair; just make sure any decoration is based on whatever you have cooked.

Aunt Fanny's BUTTERMILK SALAD

Yes, I had an aunt Fanny, my grandpa's sister-in-law on my daddy's side and she was evidently a handful, at least according to Daddy. But this woman could cook. She and Uncle Foe lived in a little town called Laurens, just south of Granny and Papa, in a small house without indoor plumbing—except there was a pump at the sink in the kitchen, a feature that fascinated me as a child. The outhouse was in the backyard right by the hog pen, which held the biggest hog I've ever seen. He guarded the moonshine still. While Uncle Foe made 'shine and kept everyone in the family happy, Aunt Fanny was the cook, and this is one of the things she made for me when I grew older. It's one of the "way back" recipes that is just good enough to dust off and use. This sweet, summery, cool salad is so refreshing it is equally welcome before or after dinner. Serve it with crackers or fruit, such as strawberries. Or, just eat it with a spoon, like we do.

SERVES 6

1 (15.25-ounce) can crushed pineapple
1 (1.5-ounce) box strawberry gelatin or ½ (3-ounce) box
2 cups buttermilk
1 (8-ounce) container frozen whipped topping, thawed
1 cup chopped pecans

1. Drain about three quarters of the liquid from the crushed pineapple. Pour the pineapple and the rest of the liquid into a small saucepan.

2. Set the saucepan over medium heat to warm, then stir in the gelatin until dissolved. Next stir in the buttermilk. Remove from the heat, pour into a bowl, and refrigerate until thick, at least 2½ hours (I let mine sit overnight).

3. Gently mix the whipped topping and pecans into the buttermilk mixture and serve.

Old-Fashioned SQUASH RELISH

Canning is one of the passed-down activities that we really have hung on to here in the South. We live season to season, and when the harvest comes in we take to putting it up—from pickles and jellies to corn and squash. I dearly love this relish on so many things, from hot dogs to collards. We can it up in the summer and have that fresh, warm taste of summer even on the coldest days of winter.

MAKES 4 PINTS

5 cups medium-diced yellow squash
2 cups chopped red onion
½ large red bell pepper, chopped
½ large green bell pepper, chopped
1 tablespoon salt
1 cup distilled white vinegar
1¼ cups sugar
½ teaspoon ground turmeric
½ teaspoon dry mustard
½ teaspoon celery seeds
½ teaspoon cornstarch

1. In a large bowl, mix together the squash, onion, bell peppers, and salt. Pour in enough ice water to cover and let sit in the refrigerator overnight.

2. Drain the vegetables and squeeze them in cheesecloth to release as much liquid from the mixture as possible.

3. In a large nonreactive pot, combine the squash mixture with the vinegar, sugar, turmeric, mustard, celery seeds, and cornstarch and bring to a boil over high heat. Reduce the heat and simmer, stirring frequently, until the vegetables have softened and the mixture starts to thicken, about 30 minutes.

4. Meanwhile, wash and sterilize (see page 28) four 1-pint canning jars.

5. Carefully scoop the mixture into the jars while still hot, leaving ⅛ inch of headspace at the top. Seal the jars and process in boiling water (see page 28).

6. Let cool and then store in a cool pantry. These are best eaten within a year of putting up. Once opened, keep in the fridge for up to a few weeks.

Cornbread SALAD

Some of you might not think to put cornbread and salad together, but hey, if it works, go with it. You ask anyone in the South who has ever been to a picnic, potluck, or family gathering and you can bet they have had this at one time or another. The crisp corn and bacon and the cool, smooth ranch dressing pair beautifully with the fresh, sweet cornbread.

SERVES 6 TO 8

¾ cup cornmeal
⅔ cup self-rising flour (I use White Lily)
¼ teaspoon baking powder
1 teaspoon salt
2 large eggs, well beaten
1 cup buttermilk
6 slices bacon
1 (1-ounce) envelope Hidden Valley ranch dressing mix
½ cup sour cream
½ cup Miracle Whip
½ cup mayonnaise (I use Duke's)
1 (12-ounce) bag frozen corn, thawed, or kernels from
6 fresh ears
1 (12-ounce) can Del Monte Fiesta corn, drained
2 (16-ounce) cans pinto beans, rinsed and drained
1 (12-ounce) bag frozen peas, thawed
1 medium red onion, diced
1 medium tomato, diced and drained in a fine-mesh sieve
2 cups shredded cheddar cheese (8 ounces)

1. Preheat the oven to 400°F. Grease an 8-inch cast-iron skillet and put it in the oven to get hot.

2. In a large bowl, combine the cornmeal, flour, baking powder, and salt. Add the eggs and buttermilk, mixing well. Pour into the hot skillet. Bake until lightly browned, 15 to 20 minutes. Let cool in the pan on a wire rack.

3. Meanwhile, in a nonstick skillet over medium heat, cook the bacon until crisp, turning once, about 12 minutes. Drain on paper towels.

4. In a small bowl, mix together the salad dressing mix, sour cream, Miracle Whip, and mayonnaise.

5. In a large bowl, mix together both types of corn, the beans, peas, onion, and tomato. Crumble in the bacon and then crumble in half of the cornbread. Mix well and then stir in the dressing mixture and half of the cheddar.

6. Transfer to a serving bowl and crumble the remaining cornbread on top. Sprinkle with the remaining cheddar and serve.

Grits and Bacon FRITTERS

Where I'm from we call these fritters, but you add bacon to anything and you can call it whatever you want. These balls have three of the four food groups in them: bacon, cheese, and grits; all that's missing is cream cheese and you can bet I'll eventually find a way to add that in, too.

MAKES ABOUT 26 FRITTERS

1 cup quick-cooking grits
4 cups whole milk
1 teaspoon salt
1½ cups shredded extra-sharp white cheddar cheese (about 6 ounces)
½ cup finely crumbled cooked bacon (about 8 slices)
2 green onions, minced
½ teaspoon black pepper
Peanut or vegetable oil, for deep-frying
2 large eggs
3 cups panko bread crumbs

1. Lightly grease an 8-inch square baking dish.

2. In a saucepan, cook the grits according to the package directions, using the milk and salt. Remove from the heat and let stand for 5 minutes. Stir in the cheddar, bacon, green onions, and pepper, stirring until the cheese is melted. Spoon the mixture into the baking dish and chill for at least 4 hours or overnight.

3. Preheat the oven to 225°F.

4. Pour oil to a depth of 3 inches in a large, heavy skillet and heat over medium-high heat to 350°F.

5. Meanwhile, in a bowl, whisk the eggs with ¼ cup water. Put the panko in a shallow bowl. Roll the grit mixture into 1½-inch balls. Dip each ball in egg wash, and then roll it in the panko.

6. Working in batches, fry the fritters until golden brown, 3 to 4 minutes. Drain on paper towels. If not serving immediately, put the fritters on a wire rack set over a baking sheet and keep them warm in the oven for up to 30 minutes. Serve warm.

FRYING NOTES

1. I use peanut oil for fish or chicken.
It is a little pricey, but it has a good, high heat level, so it doesn't smoke as badly as some other oils. If you have a peanut allergy or are cooking for someone who does, use vegetable oil; it's better than canola oil, which doesn't hold the heat as well for deep-frying.

2. I use a deep cast-iron frying pan.
It holds the heat in better than a nonstick pan.

3. I don't use a thermometer.
I test the oil by sprinkling a li'l flour in the pan. If it sizzles, the oil is ready. If it sinks, the oil is still too cool. (Daddy taught me that trick.)

4. One of the biggest tricks:
Don't drop your food into the hot oil! Instead, slide the food in and it will be safer for all. (And try not to hold your head or arms directly over the pan—oil splatter hurts!)

5. And a tip for frying bacon:
To keep the splatter and pops down, add up to $\frac{1}{4}$ cup water to the pan while it's going. The water keeps the oil from jumping.

CANNING: STERILIZING AND PROCESSING JARS

If you want your prized pickles and preserves to make it through the winter, you had better put them up properly!

To sterilize jars, put a wire rack inside a large pot. Put the jars and rings in the pot, add water to cover by at least 1 inch, and set the pot over high heat. Bring the water to a rolling boil and then boil for 10 minutes. Meanwhile, put the lids in a bowl and add boiling water to cover. Remove the jars using tongs and set upside down on a clean kitchen towel. Do the same with the lids. (Reserve the pot of boiling water.) While the jars are still warm, fill with your preserves, leaving $\frac{1}{8}$ inch free at the top for air. Wipe the rims with paper towels. Put the lids on the jars and screw the rings closed.

To process the jars, return them to the pot with the rack and boiling water. Make sure the jars are covered by an inch of water; add more if needed. Return the water to a boil and boil for 10 minutes. Using tongs, remove the jars to a clean kitchen towel to cool. Store in a cool, dry place.

Green 'Mater CHOW CHOW

As the crops are growing, we spend our days in big floppy hats digging in the dirt and whispering sweet nothings to the fruits, vegetables, and herbs we have planted. The first buds of green tomatoes are wonderful things. They mean the canning season is coming and it's time to commence the gathering of mason jars for one of the things we love to eat: 'mater chow chow. We mainly like to serve this on beans and greens because it's such a good flavor enhancer. It will definitely wake up your taste buds. I have even been told that people make sandwiches out of it! Hey, when good food is involved there are no rules.

MAKES 4 PINTS

4 medium green (unripe) tomatoes, finely chopped
2 medium red bell peppers, finely chopped
2 large Texas sweet or Vidalia onions, finely chopped
1 small head cabbage, finely shredded
½ cup pickling salt
1 tablespoon celery seeds
1 teaspoon mustard seeds
1 teaspoon dry mustard
1 teaspoon ground turmeric
3 cups distilled white vinegar
2 cups sugar

1. In a large bowl, combine the tomatoes, bell peppers, onions, cabbage, pickling salt, and 2 quarts cold water. Stir in the celery seeds, mustard seeds, dry mustard, and turmeric. Cover and let stand for 1 hour.

2. Meanwhile, wash and sterilize (see the opposite page) four 1-pint canning jars.

3. In a large nonreactive pot, combine the vinegar, sugar, and vegetable mixture. Bring to a simmer over medium heat and cook, uncovered, until the vegetables have softened, about 25 minutes.

4. Carefully scoop the mixture into the jars while still hot, leaving ⅛ inch of headspace at the top. Seal the jars and process in boiling water (see the opposite page).

5. Let cool and then store in a cool pantry. These are best eaten within a year of putting up. Once opened, keep in the fridge for up to a few weeks.

Chicken and Dumplings like
Mama Made, page 42

YARD-
BIRD

(Or "chicken" for the city folk)

I sure do treasure this lovely li'l clucking animal. We started with three in our backyard, and at the time of this writing we're up to thirty by my count. I'm really not sure where they all came from (insert a joke here about when a mama chicken and a daddy chicken fall in love . . .). We call our house the Hillbilly Hideaway—aka "The Home for Wayward Poultry." Now, before you get your overalls in a twist, no, we don't kill our chickens and eat them. I use our hens' eggs in baking and buy my chicken at the store like everyone else. Nothing makes a better cake than a good old yard egg, and I do like my birds destined for the oven or skillet to have been free-range, too.

THE BEST FRIED CHICKEN YOU'LL EVER EAT

HOT FRIED CHICKEN (FOR EFFIE'S HEAT LEVEL)

Faked-Out Fried Chicken

HOMEMADE CREAM OF CHICKEN SOUP

LEMON-HERB CHICKEN

Chicken and Family Favorite Holiday Dressing

CHICKEN AND DUMPLINGS LIKE MAMA MADE

SLOW-COOKED HAWAIIAN REDNECK CHICKEN

Ginger-Lime Chicken Wings

BOURBON AND COKE WINGS

WHOLE ROASTED SPICED CHICKEN

The Best Fried Chicken
YOU'LL EVER EAT

My daddy made the best fried chicken in the world. His closely guarded secret? Season the chicken and then let it sit overnight in the fridge. The seasonings penetrate the bird and help keep it moist inside and crisp outside. Hot sauce is key here, but don't worry: Most of the heat will cook out leaving just this amazing flavor.

SERVES 8

4 pounds bone-in, skin-on chicken pieces
Morton Season-All Seasoned Salt
Salt and black pepper
2 large eggs
1½ cups buttermilk
¼ cup hot sauce (or to taste; I use Texas Pete)
2½ cups all-purpose flour
2 tablespoons cornstarch
Peanut or vegetable oil, for deep-frying

1. Season the chicken pieces on all sides with Season-All and salt and pepper. Put the chicken on a platter, cover, and refrigerate overnight.

2. In a large bowl, whisk together the eggs, buttermilk, and hot sauce. Add the chicken pieces and let sit for 30 minutes, or until the chicken reaches room temperature.

3. In a pie pan, mix together the flour, cornstarch, 2 tablespoons salt, and 2 teaspoons pepper.

4. Pour oil to a depth of 4 inches in a large, heavy-bottomed pot and heat over medium-high heat to 340°F. Test with a dash of flour—if the flour sizzles on contact, the oil is ready.

5. Taking one piece of chicken at a time, dip it in the buttermilk mixture, and then coat the chicken in the flour mixture, shaking off the excess.

6. Fry the chicken in batches until golden brown, 6 to 8 minutes per side, so 12 to 16 minutes per piece. Dark meat takes longer to cook than white meat. In either case, don't dry out your chicken!

7. Drain the chicken on paper towels or a flat brown paper bag. Serve hot or let cool and then refrigerate for a picnic.

Hot Fried Chicken
(FOR EFFIE'S HEAT LEVEL)

As many of you know, ever since *The American Baking Competition* Effie has been one of my closest friends. I love her like a sister. She's an amazing wife, mom, and cook—and she has a tolerance level for spicy food that keeps me flat-out in awe. Effie happens to live in Nashville, the home of Hattie B's Hot Chicken. If you ever get the chance to visit her city, put that place on your list. It's that good. If you're in Effie's camp and like your chicken hot hot hot!, this one's for you.

SERVES 6

4 cups shortening (I use Crisco)
3½ pounds bone-in, skin-on chicken pieces
Salt and black pepper
3 large eggs
½ cup whole milk
½ cup hot sauce (I use Texas Pete)
1½ cups all-purpose flour
1 tablespoon garlic powder
1 tablespoon onion powder
1½ tablespoons cayenne pepper
1 tablespoon paprika, plus more for serving

1. In a deep-fryer or a large, heavy-bottomed pot, heat the shortening to 375°F.

2. Season the chicken pieces on all sides with salt and black pepper.

3. In a shallow bowl, whisk together the eggs, milk, hot sauce, and 1 teaspoon salt. In a separate shallow bowl, mix together the flour, garlic powder, onion powder, cayenne, paprika, and 1 tablespoon black pepper.

4. Working in batches, coat each piece of chicken in the flour and spice mixture. Dip in the egg mixture, then return the chicken to the flour mixture for a second coat. Once coated, put immediately into the hot shortening and fry, turning once, until deep golden brown, 12 to 15 minutes.

5. Drain the chicken on paper towels or a flat brown paper bag. Sprinkle with a dusting of paprika before serving.

Faked-Out FRIED CHICKEN

Now before y'all think I'm talking about tofu, just calm down! I'm bringing you cornflake-crusted baked chicken. There's no oil and it's healthy, so you can save room for a slice of pie.

SERVES 4

2 cups crushed cornflakes
1 tablespoon garlic powder
1 tablespoon poultry seasoning
Salt and black pepper
4 large egg whites
4 boneless, skinless chicken breast halves

1. Preheat the oven to 375°F. Lightly grease a baking dish.

2. In a large bowl, combine the cornflakes, garlic powder, poultry seasoning, and salt and pepper to taste. Put the egg whites in a shallow bowl and whisk them lightly.

3. Coat each piece of chicken with the egg whites and then drag them through the cornflake mixture.

4. Put the chicken in the baking dish and bake until golden brown and cooked through, 25 to 30 minutes.

Homemade
CREAM OF CHICKEN SOUP

Often (particularly in the South) a casserole or a one-pot meal will call for a can or two of cream of chicken soup. But sometimes it's worth the extra time to make it from scratch. You can bet this quick and easy cream soup is better than that canned stuff. (The same goes for cream of mushroom and cream of celery; see pages 149 and 148 for the recipes.) Freeze it in 1½-cup portions to deploy at will.

MAKES 6 CUPS (SERVES 6)

2 boneless, skinless chicken breast halves,
or 1½ cups finely chopped leftover cooked chicken
4 tablespoons (½ stick) unsalted butter
¼ cup all-purpose flour
1 cup heavy cream
3 cups chicken broth
¼ teaspoon poultry seasoning
½ teaspoon dried thyme
½ teaspoon dried basil
¼ teaspoon salt
1 teaspoon black pepper

1. In a large saucepan, combine the chicken with water to cover. Bring to a simmer over high heat and cook the chicken until cooked through, about 20 minutes. (Skip this step if you are using leftover cooked chicken.) Drain and chop the meat into very fine pieces. Measure out 1½ cups for this recipe.

2. In a Dutch oven or large pot over medium heat, melt the butter. Slowly whisk in the flour, whisking constantly. You are making a roux and it will become thick very fast. Slowly whisk in the cream and broth. Keep whisking until the mixture is thickened and bubbling, 6 to 8 minutes. Reduce the heat so that the sauce simmers.

3. Stir in the chicken, poultry seasoning, thyme, basil, salt, and pepper and cook to heat through.

4. Using an immersion blender (or in batches in a stand blender), carefully blend the soup until smooth.

Lemon-Herb CHICKEN

Lemon is one of those flavors that complements everything it touches, and it's a great match with chicken. This recipe is loaded with lots of bright citrus flavor thanks to a quick fresh lemon juice marinade and a lemon-herb seasoning. Daddy would make this for me whenever something good happened. It was his "let's celebrate" food. We never went out to eat on those special occasions; instead he'd cook for us. And I was always right there at his heels, mainly because the phone was on the wall in the kitchen and I could help him and talk on the phone at the same time. Daddy would serve this with rice or mashed potatoes; I'd add one of my veggie recipes from the sides chapter, too.

SERVES 6 TO 8

12 small boneless, skinless chicken breast tenders (1½ pounds total)
½ cup fresh lemon juice
1 cup all-purpose flour
Dash of paprika
Pinch each of salt and black pepper
1 tablespoon lemon-herb seasoning
Peanut or vegetable oil, for deep-frying

1. Rinse the chicken with cold water, pat dry with a paper towel, and lightly poke holes in them with a fork. Put the strips in a medium bowl and add the lemon juice. Let the chicken soak in the lemon juice for about 15 minutes.

2. In another medium bowl, stir together the flour, paprika, salt, pepper, and ½ tablespoon of the lemon-herb seasoning.

3. Drain the chicken and coat the strips well with the flour mixture. (You may have to do this twice, to be sure of a good coating.)

4. Pour oil to a depth of 1½ inches in a large, heavy skillet and heat over medium-high heat to 350°F. Test with a dash of flour—if the flour sizzles on contact, the oil is ready. Once the oil is hot, add the chicken strips. Cook, turning once, until golden brown with a slightly yellow tint, about 9 minutes.

5. Drain the chicken on paper towels. While still hot, sprinkle the chicken with the remaining ½ tablespoon lemon-herb seasoning.

Chicken and Family Favorite
HOLIDAY DRESSING

The first thing you need to know about this recipe is that it's a great weeknight meal, especially if you do things my way. For one, half of it is already made—hallelujah rotisserie chicken! And two, I always have dressing in the freezer because I believe that it's not just for the holidays. You can't tell me that at some point in the spring you don't get a hankering for some Thanksgiving! Well, here's your fix-me-up.

SERVES 6

1 (3-pound) store-bought rotisserie chicken
3 cups Family Favorite Holiday Dressing (page 124)
Chicken Gravy (recipe follows)

Tear the chicken into pieces and put on plates with a scoop of dressing. Cover with gravy and serve.

CHICKEN GRAVY

MAKES ABOUT 2½ CUPS

3 tablespoons unsalted butter
3 tablespoons all-purpose flour
2 (12-ounce) cans chicken stock

1. In a saucepan over medium-high heat, melt the butter. Whisk in the flour and cook, stirring constantly, until incorporated and lightly golden, about 3 minutes.

2. Reduce the heat to medium-low and add the chicken stock a bit at a time, whisking constantly. When thickened, about 5 minutes, remove from the heat and serve.

Chicken and Dumplings
LIKE MAMA MADE

Mama was a great cook and every time I make one of her recipes, even if I go step-by-step, it never ends up tasting quite like hers did. There must be something about a mama's cooking—my daughter, Sarablake, says she can't make things taste as good as mine, either. It's all in a mama's love, and my mama put all of that into this dish, a Southern classic that everyone makes in her own way.

SERVES 8

CHICKEN

1 (3-pound) whole chicken, cut into 8 pieces
3 large carrots, diced
3 celery stalks, diced
1 medium onion, diced
3 chicken bouillon cubes
½ teaspoon black pepper

DUMPLINGS

2 cups all-purpose flour, plus more for rolling the dough
½ teaspoon baking soda
½ teaspoon kosher salt
3 tablespoons shortening (I use Crisco)
¾ cup buttermilk

1. Prepare the chicken: In a large stockpot, combine the chicken, carrots, celery, onion, bouillon cubes, and pepper. Add enough water to cover the chicken and vegetables (at least 2 quarts) and bring to a boil over high heat. Reduce to a simmer and cook until the chicken is cooked through, about 30 minutes. Remove the chicken from the broth and set the chicken aside to cool.

2. Strain the broth into a bowl, reserving the vegetables. Measure out 6 cups of the broth and pour into a Dutch oven. (Reserve any leftover broth for soup or gravy. It'll keep in the fridge for a week or in the freezer for months.) Add the vegetables to the pot, too.

3. Make the dumplings: In a medium bowl, stir together the flour, baking soda, and salt. Cut the shortening

into the flour mixture using a pastry blender, 2 knives, or your fingertips. Add the buttermilk slowly, stirring gently until a dough forms.

4. Flour your work surface, then roll out the dough until it is about ¼ inch thick. Cut the dough into 1-inch-wide strips that are about 8 inches long, then cut the strips in half crosswise. Put the dough strips on wax paper and let dry for about 30 minutes to firm up slightly.

5. Meanwhile, remove and discard the skin and bones from the chicken and shred the meat into bite-size chunks. Add the chicken chunks to the broth in the Dutch oven and bring the mixture to a simmer.

6. Add the dough strips to the broth and simmer until the dough has expanded, 6 to 8 minutes. Serve hot.

Slow-Cooked
HAWAIIAN REDNECK CHICKEN

In my family, we love Hawaiian pizza, dotted with pineapple, and this is almost like it. It's a li'l sweet and savory and very simple to make. This set-it-and-forget-it meal may just take you to the islands. I say cook it when it's cold outside and you need to visualize sun-kissed beaches to keep your spirits up.

SERVES 4

Cooking spray
4 boneless, skinless chicken breast halves
1 (20-ounce) can pineapple rings, drained and juice reserved
1 green bell pepper, chopped
3 tablespoons soy sauce
Juice of 1 lemon
2 tablespoons light brown sugar
2 tablespoons cornstarch
½ teaspoon ground ginger
½ teaspoon salt
½ teaspoon black pepper
Cooked white rice, for serving

1. Coat the insert of a slow cooker with cooking spray. Add the chicken to the pot. Arrange the pineapple rings and bell pepper on top of the chicken.

2. In a small bowl, whisk together the pineapple juice, soy sauce, lemon juice, brown sugar, cornstarch, ginger, salt, and pepper until the brown sugar and cornstarch are dissolved. Pour the pineapple juice mixture into the pot.

3. Cover and cook on high for 2½ to 3 hours or on low for 4 to 6 hours.

4. Serve over rice.

Ginger-Lime CHICKEN WINGS

The secret here is all in the overnight marinating. Spicy ginger and tart lime make a great pair—and a nice change-up from regular hot wings. I think this is what the food on the islands would taste like—I myself have never been, but I'll get there one day!

SERVES 6

1 pound whole chicken wings
1 cup soy sauce
¼ cup olive oil
1 tablespoon fresh lime juice
2 tablespoons minced fresh ginger
6 garlic cloves, smashed
1 bunch green onions, chopped
Cooking spray

1. Put the chicken in a large resealable plastic bag. In a small bowl, mix together ½ cup water, the soy sauce, olive oil, lime juice, ginger, garlic, and green onions. Pour the mixture into the bag with the wings. Refrigerate the wings for 2 hours or overnight.

2. Preheat the oven to 350°F. Line a baking sheet with foil and coat with cooking spray.

3. Drain the wings and spread out on the prepared baking sheet. Bake, flipping them halfway through, until the wings are cooked through and the skin is crispy, about 25 minutes.

From top: Bourbon and Coke Wings and
Ginger-Lime Chicken Wings (page 45)

Bourbon and Coke WINGS

Oh, have mercy, I love me some Coca-Cola. You put a little bourbon in it and my hubby is a happy man, so I thought one day, Why not try that combo on wings? Most really good recipes are created from a desire for something a little bit different but using whatever you have on hand. I'm not a drinker, and truthfully Mark really isn't, either. I think I've been using the same bottle of Jim Beam since I gave it to him eight years ago! So, waste not, want not—we have it and I might as well find ways to use it. That's how these awesome chicken wings were born.

SERVES 8 TO 10

3 pounds chicken wing drumettes
3 tablespoons olive oil
Salt and black pepper
1 cup Coca-Cola
¼ cup bourbon
3 tablespoons hot sauce (I use Texas Pete)
3 tablespoons honey
2 tablespoons unsalted butter

1. Preheat the oven to 450°F. Line a rimmed baking sheet with foil.

2. Arrange the chicken on the baking sheet. Drizzle with the oil, turning to coat. Season with salt and pepper. Bake for 20 minutes. Carefully pour out any liquid that has accumulated and return to the oven. Bake until the chicken is a deep, golden brown and super crispy, about 5 minutes longer.

3. Meanwhile, in a small saucepan, combine the Coke, bourbon, hot sauce, honey, and butter. Bring the mixture to a boil over high heat, then reduce the heat to medium-low and simmer until the sauce reduces to a thick glaze, about 30 minutes.

4. Remove the wings from the oven and brush generously with the glaze, then return the wings to the oven and bake until sticky, about 5 minutes longer.

Whole Roasted SPICED CHICKEN

Rednecks can't live by fried chicken alone, although I sometimes think I wouldn't mind trying. But we eat chicken more than red meat and so I'm always looking for a good recipe I can run with. This one comes out juicy, deeply browned, and full of aromatic spices. The roasting bag keeps it moist and makes the cleanup easy. Swap seasonings in and out as you see fit to customize this bird for yourself. And you can even make chicken salad out of the leftovers.

SERVES 4

1 tablespoon salt
2 teaspoons smoked paprika
1½ teaspoons black pepper
1½ teaspoons Chinese 5-spice powder
1 teaspoon dried thyme
1 teaspoon onion powder
½ teaspoon garlic powder
1 (3-pound) whole chicken
2 tablespoons vegetable oil
2 large onions, roughly chopped

1. In a small bowl, mix together the salt, paprika, pepper, 5-spice powder, thyme, onion powder, and garlic powder. Rub the outside of the chicken with the oil and sprinkle the mixed spices over the skin until the chicken is covered. Put 1 chopped onion into the cavity of the chicken. Put the chicken in a large roasting bag and refrigerate overnight.

2. Preheat the oven to 350°F.

3. Put the remaining onion in the roasting bag with the chicken then put the bag on a baking pan. Bake until golden and cooked through, about 2 hours.

4. Let sit for 10 minutes before removing the chicken from the bag and carving the chicken.

Mac-and-Cheese Burgers,
page 58

BURGERS

& Bryson

BBQ FAVORITES

And other picnic table must-haves

There's nothing I love more than barbecue. OK, maybe chocolate, or coffee, or doughnuts. . . . But barbecue is one of the things that us Southerners can really lay claim to. We do BBQ better than any other part of the country. We compete at it, we swap plates of it, and we take some of our best secrets for it to our graves. It's serious business for some, but I think it should be fun and easy, a reason to gather the family and enjoy a meal outside. We throw a fine picnic, with or without smoked meat (but preferably with). Personally, I'm indebted to our pastime as it's one of the reasons my husband proposed. He just loves my pork butt.

BBQ PORK BUTT (IN THE OVEN)

BACON AND CHEESE STUFFED BURGERS

Blue Cheese Spicy BBQ Burgers

MAC-AND-CHEESE BURGERS

GRANNY-STYLE MAC AND CHEESE

Ribs at Home

OVEN HONEY RIBS

BLUEBERRY BBQ SAUCE

Sweet Heat BBQ Sauce

SLAW FOR THE FAMILY BARBECUE

FRIED CORN ON THE COB

Bacon BBQ'd Baked Beans

Oven Honey Ribs, page 62

SHREDDED PORK SANDWICHES

Make the pork butt recipe and then toss the meat in your favorite sauce. Spoon the sauced pork over buttered and toasted hamburger buns and serve warm—and I also like coleslaw (see page 67) on my pork sandwiches.

BBQ Pork Butt (IN THE OVEN)

When I'm making this, Mark always comes up and says, "Every good butt deserves a good rub." (It's a phrase also seen on signs at some good BBQ joints.) So to start this recipe, make a good rub. And when you're choosing your pork butt, always look for good marbling. I go for one that's 4 to 7 pounds. If you don't have a grill, don't worry; this one is roasted in the oven. No one ever complains about that in my house.

SERVES 14 TO 16

RUB

½ cup packed light brown sugar

2 tablespoons paprika

1½ teaspoons onion powder

1½ teaspoons garlic powder

1 teaspoon dry mustard

1 teaspoon ground cumin

½ teaspoon ground ginger

½ teaspoon salt

1 (4- to 7-pound) bone-in pork butt

1. Make the rub: In a large bowl, combine all of the rub ingredients and mix well.

2. Put the pork butt in the bowl, rub the seasoning all over the pork, and let it sit uncovered in the refrigerator for 2 hours, or cover the pork butt and refrigerate overnight.

3. Thirty minutes before you begin to cook, take the pork out of the refrigerator and let the butt come to room temperature. This will keep the meat tender.

4. Preheat the oven to 325°F.

5. Put the pork butt in a roasting pan, cover with heavy-duty foil, leaving a little room to spare, and roast until the pork is so tender it pulls away from the bone, about 3 hours.

6. Remove the butt from the oven and let rest for 30 minutes. Then, using a fork, pull the meat away from the bone and into shreds.

Bacon and Cheese
STUFFED BURGERS

I have traveled across the country and Daddy taught me to look for the little mom-and-pop burger joints, because they're the best. They put so much love into the food and you can taste it. I had this particular burger in Virginia while traveling with him in my younger days. As I recall, from the first moment I bit into one of these it was like grease-dripping-from-my-elbows, cheesy heaven. This burger qualifies as food porn in my book.

SERVES 4

2 slices bacon, cooked
2 pounds 80% lean ground beef
1 teaspoon Worcestershire sauce
½ teaspoon onion powder
½ teaspoon salt
½ teaspoon black pepper
½ cup shredded cheddar cheese (about 2 ounces)
4 large seeded hamburger buns, split

1. In a nonstick skillet over medium heat, cook the bacon until crispy, about 12 minutes. Drain on paper towels and then chop the bacon into small pieces.

2. In a large bowl, use your hands to thoroughly mix together the beef, Worcestershire sauce, onion powder, salt, and pepper.

3. Preheat the grill or a grill pan to medium-high.

4. Dampen your hands and form the seasoned meat into 8 equal balls. Gently press the balls into patties that are about ½ inch thick. Put 2 tablespoons cheddar and one-quarter of the bacon in the middle of each of 4 patties and top each with a naked patty. Press together.

5. Grill the burgers for about 5 minutes on each side for medium, or to desired doneness. Remove the burgers and let rest on a clean plate while you warm the buns on the grill. Sandwich those burgers on up between the buns and chow down!

Blue Cheese SPICY BBQ BURGERS

Blue cheese and spice on a burger has got to be a major untapped resource. If heat is not your thing, you can omit it, but it's not enough to light you up; just enough to warm you up a touch.

SERVES 4

1¾ pounds 90% lean ground beef
1 large egg
¼ medium onion, finely diced
2 tablespoons Worcestershire sauce
2 tablespoons hot sauce (I use Texas Pete)
2½ teaspoons garlic powder
1¼ teaspoons cayenne pepper
Salt and black pepper
½ cup plain bread crumbs
1½ cups crumbled blue cheese
4 hamburger buns, split

1. In a large bowl, combine the beef, egg, onion, Worcestershire sauce, hot sauce, garlic powder, cayenne, and a pinch each of salt and pepper. Sprinkle in the bread crumbs to soak up extra moisture and mix well.

2. With damp hands, divide the mixture into 8 equal balls. Flatten the balls out into patties ⅜ inch thick and 4 to 5 inches in diameter. Put one quarter of the blue cheese in the middle of one of the patties and top with a naked patty. Press together. Repeat with the remaining patties and cheese.

3. Preheat the grill or a grill pan to medium-high.

4. Grill until done to your liking, about 7 minutes per side for medium. Set the burgers aside, covered with foil to stay warm. Warm the buns on the grill and serve the burgers on the buns.

Mac-and-Cheese BURGERS

My crunchy, gooey patties of mac and cheese perched on top of a beef burger will make you dance. You put your mac and cheese on your burger and you turn yourself around—that's what it's all about! This one will even make the kids put down their cell phones and converse. You can use your favorite mac and cheese recipe in these burgers—or my granny's (see opposite page).

SERVES 4

2 pounds 80% lean ground beef
Salt and black pepper
1⅓ cups cooked mac and cheese, cooled
2 tablespoons mayonnaise (I use Duke's)
All-purpose flour, for coating
¼ cup peanut or vegetable oil
4 onion hamburger buns, split
4 lettuce leaves
4 large sweet onion slices
4 tomato slices

1. With damp hands, form the beef into 4 patties each ½ inch thick, and season on both sides with salt and pepper.

2. Form the mac and cheese into 4 patties each about 3 inches across. Spread both sides of the mac-and-cheese patties with the mayonnaise and then sprinkle a little flour on the tops and bottoms of the patties.

3. Preheat the grill or a grill pan to medium-high.

4. Grill the burgers to your liking, about 4 minutes on each side for medium. Set the burgers aside, covered with foil to stay warm.

5. In a skillet over medium-high heat, heat the oil. Very gently fry the mac-and-cheese patties until slightly browned, about 2 minutes. Then turn and fry the other sides, 2 minutes longer.

6. Warm the buns on the grill and then fill them each with a beef patty, a mac-and-cheese patty, lettuce, onion, and tomato.

Granny-Style MAC AND CHEESE

My granny made the best mac and cheese in the world, but I'm sure everybody's granny does! The old-school way of making this dish has always been the best, so smooth and cheesy. This addictive, from-scratch version of the childhood favorite is fit for grown-ups, too.

SERVES 12

1 (16-ounce) box elbow macaroni

2 large eggs

1 (12-ounce) can evaporated milk

10 tablespoons (1¼ sticks) unsalted butter, melted

1 teaspoon salt

1 teaspoon black pepper

4 cups shredded extra-sharp cheddar cheese (16 ounces)

1. Preheat the oven to 350°F.

2. Cook the pasta according to the package directions until just underdone (you don't want it mushy now because it will absorb more liquid in the oven). Drain and set aside in a 9 × 13-inch baking dish.

3. In a bowl, whisk together the eggs, evaporated milk, butter, salt, and pepper. Stir in the cheddar. Pour the cheese mixture over the cooked pasta and stir to combine.

4. Bake until golden brown on top and bubbling, 40 to 45 minutes.

Ribs AT HOME

My husband is generally more of a beef eater, but pork ribs are a little easier to master and y'all know me—I'm all about the easy way to good food! These are tender ribs that will not fall off the bone into your lap, which is the perfect texture for a championship barbecue—even if I cheat a little and start mine in the oven. (Yes, that's right; if a judge takes a bite and the whole slab of meat falls off, they will disqualify it!)

SERVES 4

RUB

½ cup packed light brown sugar
¼ cup paprika
1 tablespoon kosher salt
1 tablespoon black pepper
1 tablespoon chili powder
2 teaspoons garlic powder
2 teaspoons onion powder
¼ teaspoon cayenne pepper

2 full racks (about 6 pounds total) pork spareribs (not baby back)
2 cups apple cider
Barbecue sauce, homemade (pages 65 and 66) or store-bought

1. Make the rub: In a large bowl, combine all of the rub ingredients and mix well.

2. Rub the seasoning all over the pork ribs, then wrap in plastic wrap and refrigerate overnight.

3. Thirty minutes before you begin to cook, take the pork out of the refrigerator and bring to room temperature. This will keep the meat tender.

4. Preheat the oven to 350°F. Line 2 large baking sheets with foil.

5. Arrange the pork ribs on the baking pans and bake for 1½ hours.

6. Preheat a grill to about 220°F. Meanwhile, soak 2 cups of wood chips in cold water. I like Jack Daniel's oakwood chips, made from old whiskey barrels, but pick whatever you like.

7. Now you're ready to finish the ribs and pack in that smoky flavor. Drain the wood chips and wrap in foil. Poke a few holes in the top of the foil packet and add to one side of the grill. (Alternatively, if your grill has a smoker box, you can skip the foil and put the chips directly in the box.) Put the ribs on the other part of the grill and brush them with the apple cider. Close the lid and let them smoke until the meat pulls away from the bone, about 1 hour, brushing them again with the cider halfway through. If the meat is not pulling away from the bone after an hour, continue to smoke, checking them every 15 minutes thereafter.

8. Brush the ribs down with your favorite barbecue sauce and serve.

Oven Honey RIBS

I had an old friend who taught me this recipe before he passed. He loved him some BBQ and he was great at making it; whether on the grill or in the oven, he had the touch. Honey and BBQ go hand in hand and this recipe makes a sweet, tangy, sticky rib with a bit of kick to it at the end. The malty flavor from the beer is as good as malt vinegar on fries at an Irish pub.

SERVES 4

RUB

1 tablespoon kosher salt
1 tablespoon granulated onion
1 tablespoon granulated garlic
1 teaspoon smoked paprika
1 teaspoon black pepper

2 full racks (about 6 pounds total) baby back ribs

BARBECUE SAUCE

1 cup ketchup
⅔ cup Worcestershire sauce
⅔ cup packed light brown sugar
½ teaspoon hot sauce (I use Texas Pete)
1 teaspoon black pepper
1 teaspoon salt
1 teaspoon smoked paprika
1 teaspoon chili powder
2 tablespoons yellow mustard (I use French's)
1 tablespoon liquid smoke flavoring
1 teaspoon minced garlic
¼ cup all-purpose flour
1 (12-ounce) bottle amber ale
½ cup honey

1. Make the rub: In a small bowl, combine all of the rub ingredients.

2. Sprinkle the tops of the racks with 2 heaping tablespoons of the rub. Turn and sprinkle the bottom surface of the racks with the remaining rub. Wrap in plastic wrap and refrigerate for at least 8 hours or overnight.

3. Make the barbecue sauce: In a large, heavy-bottomed pot, combine all of the sauce ingredients. Whisk until smooth. Bring to a simmer over low heat and cook, stirring occasionally, until thickened, about 30 minutes.

4. Preheat the oven to 250°F. Line a baking pan or sheet with foil.

5. Remove the plastic wrap from the racks and arrange them on the baking pan or sheet. Cover the pan with foil and bake the ribs until the meat starts to pull away from the end of the rib, about 3½ hours.

6. Remove the ribs from the oven and let rest for 10 minutes. Remove the foil and drain off any accumulated liquid. Brush both sides of ribs with the barbecue sauce, then return them to the oven and cook, uncovered, until darkened in color, 30 minutes longer.

Blueberry BBQ SAUCE

Now, you have to admit this recipe sounds a bit strange; it may not be something you see every day. But we do love our blueberries down here and we use them just about any way we can. So, one summer a few years back I was messing around in the kitchen with loads of sweet-tart fresh blueberries and came up with this barbecue sauce—and wouldn't you know it, I loved it. I like to use it on summer ribs, pork butt—or just on plain white bread!

MAKES ABOUT 2½ CUPS

2 teaspoons vegetable oil
¼ cup minced onion
¼ cup ketchup
¼ cup rice vinegar
⅓ cup granulated sugar
3 tablespoons packed light brown sugar
3 tablespoons Dijon mustard
1 teaspoon hot sauce (I use Texas Pete)
¼ cup bourbon or whiskey (Jim, Jack, or Johnny will work, but it's optional)
2 cups fresh or frozen blueberries
Salt and black pepper

1. Heat the oil in a saucepan over medium heat. Add the onion and cook until translucent, about 5 minutes. Add the ketchup, vinegar, granulated sugar, brown sugar, mustard, hot sauce, and bourbon (if using) and bring to a simmer. Add the blueberries and simmer over low heat, stirring until thickened, about 10 minutes.

2. Puree the sauce in a blender or food processor until smooth. Pass it through a fine-mesh sieve and season with salt and pepper to taste.

3. Serve warm or at room temperature. Once cool, the sauce can be kept in an airtight container in the refrigerator for several weeks.

Sweet Heat BBQ SAUCE

I have an overactive sweet tooth, and a good sense for all things sweet, even in the savory. Put a little spice in with it and, well, then it screams to me. When I was growing up, Daddy always put a touch of heat on everything. As he said, "we're full-blooded Irish, Frannie; you can handle anything." So be brave, my BBQers: Walk on the wild side and try this sauce sweetened with brown sugar and maple syrup and spiked with hot sauce and chipotle.

MAKES ABOUT 4 CUPS

```
2 cups ketchup
½ cup spicy brown mustard
½ cup cider vinegar
3 tablespoons hot sauce (I use Texas Pete)
2 tablespoons maple syrup
1 tablespoon Worcestershire sauce
⅔ cup packed light brown sugar
2 tablespoons dried onion
¼ teaspoon ground chipotle
3 tablespoons unsalted butter or margarine
```

1. In a heavy saucepan, stir together the ketchup, mustard, vinegar, hot sauce, maple syrup, Worcestershire sauce, brown sugar, dried onion, and ground chipotle. Bring to a simmer over medium heat and cook until thickened, about 20 minutes.

2. Remove from the heat, stir in the butter, and set aside to cool. Serve at room temperature. This sauce can be stored in an airtight container in the refrigerator for several weeks, if not longer.

Slaw FOR THE FAMILY BARBECUE

Now, before you try this recipe, take note that I make a mayonnaise-based slaw, not a vinegar-based slaw. We like a heavily sauced slaw where I come from.

SERVES 8

¾ cup mayonnaise (I use Duke's)
⅓ cup sugar
⅓ cup buttermilk
3 tablespoons distilled white vinegar
¾ teaspoon salt
½ teaspoon black pepper
1 head cabbage, finely shredded
1 large carrot, finely shredded

In a large bowl, whisk together the mayonnaise, sugar, buttermilk, vinegar, salt, and pepper. Stir in the cabbage and carrot. Cover and refrigerate for at least 20 minutes and up to overnight before serving.

THE PERFECT SC BBQ PARTY

A BBQ menu at my house includes: ribs, pork sandwiches, coleslaw, potato salad, deviled eggs, Texas garlic toast, fresh sliced tomatoes drizzled with balsamic, roasted corn, baked beans—and hot dogs for the kids. Here are a few tips of mine for pulling off a great outdoor meal:

1. Make the salads the day before.
The flavors will have a chance to get to know one another and it'll all just taste better.

2. Corn should always be fresh, not canned.
Silver Queen is my go-to variety. Go to weekend outdoor markets and farm stands and get to know your local farmers. The small farmers grow the best food (unless you have your own garden, which is even better).

3. Have the meat marinated and ready to go—and then let it reach room temperature!
If you throw cold ribs or pork butt onto the grill or into the oven, the tendons will tighten up and the meat can get tough. This is true for any meat you're cooking, from chops to steak or hamburger.

4. Don't forget dessert!
A homemade pie is always nice—as are individual custards or trifles in mason jars.

Fried CORN ON THE COB

Fried, boiled, roasted, on or off the cob, corn is one of the things we can all agree on. You can't have a family get-together down here without it. Sometimes I just boil corn as a snack. But if you then go on to fry it, it's so good it makes you wanna slap somebody. The crispy browned bits of sweet corn make this extra step worth doing.

SERVES 6

6 ears corn, husked and halved crosswise
2 tablespoons bacon drippings or melted butter
2 teaspoons sugar
½ teaspoon salt
¼ teaspoon black pepper

1. Bring a large pot of water to a boil. Boil the corn for 10 minutes, then drain and set aside until cool enough to handle.

2. Insert a heavy bamboo stick into one side of each of the cobs (to use as a handle) or use metal skewers. Brush the corn with the bacon drippings and sprinkle with the sugar, salt, and pepper.

3. In a cast-iron pan over medium heat, cook the ears of corn, rolling them as they heat up. The corn will become puffy and golden brown, about 3 minutes. Let cool slightly before serving. These can be made ahead of time then reheated for a party.

Bacon *BBQ'd* BAKED BEANS

Everyone I know has their own special trick for baked beans, and some would say I'm going about it all wrong. But I'm a firm believer that a li'l pig makes everything better. It's just too bad we can't raise pigs that are already BBQ flavored. . . . Now that would be great! In the meantime, try some pig with the beans; you won't be disappointed.

SERVES 12

4 (16-ounce) cans pork and beans
1 large onion, chopped
½ cup packed light brown sugar
¼ cup barbecue sauce, homemade (pages 65 and 66)
or store-bought
2 tablespoons honey
½ tablespoon Dijon mustard
2 tablespoons garlic powder
Salt and black pepper
1 pound bacon

1. Preheat the oven to 350°F.

2. In a large bowl, stir together the beans, onion, brown sugar, barbecue sauce, honey, mustard, and garlic powder and season to taste with salt and pepper. Pour the beans into a 9 × 13-inch baking dish. Arrange the bacon slices across the top of the beans.

3. Bake until the beans are bubbling and the bacon is cooked and slightly crispy, 35 to 40 minutes.

Blue Ribbon Stuffed Pork Loin,
page 74

MEAT, MEAT & a Li'l Meat

A carnivore's delight

Hi, my name is Francine and I am a carnivore. I eat meat of some sort at every meal. I'm not saying that meat is *all* there is to eat on the table; we just love it on the menu. Mark says meat always has a place right beside the 'taters, and I did marry a meat-and-taters man. (In fact, it was a full two years before I could get him to eat a meal that didn't have meat in it!) This chapter includes some of the favorites in my house, some recipes that have been passed down in my family, and some that are newer discoveries.

BLUE RIBBON STUFFED PORK LOIN

Pork Chop Casserole

SARA'S PORK CHOPS

CORNED BEEF HASH

GOLDEN CUBE STEAKS

Meatloaf to Stop a Man in His Tracks

CHEESEBURGER PIE

HAMBURGER STEW

Cheeseburger-without-the-Bun Soup

BEEF CRUNCH BAKE

FRIED LIVER WITH ONION GRAVY

Squirrel Pot Pie

Blue Ribbon STUFFED PORK LOIN

This is the recipe that started it all—or at least my competitive streak when it came to food, which I still have thirty years later! Daddy pushed then sixteen-year-old me to enter my first food competition and to open my mind up to combinations that you wouldn't think would work. So there I was at the Wakulla County Youth Swine Show with this pork recipe, which won first place in the pork category. From that moment on I was hooked. It takes a few more steps than just getting in the kitchen, but it's so worth it. I still make this today for special occasions, sometimes with cherries, blackberries, and apple in the stuffing. The good thing about pork is it's a sweet meat on its own and it pairs well with fruits, so try it and let your imagination run wild.

SERVES 8 TO 10

1 cup apple juice
1 cup dried apricots
2 tablespoons unsalted butter
2 tablespoons olive oil
4 celery stalks, diced
1 medium onion, chopped
2 garlic cloves, chopped
2 tablespoons chopped fresh parsley
1 tablespoon chopped fresh basil
2 pinches of kosher salt
2 pinches of black pepper
4 cups herbed stuffing mix
1 tablespoon Worcestershire sauce
2 pounds boneless pork loin
1 (8-ounce) jar apricot preserves
⅓ cup balsamic vinegar
2 tablespoons light brown sugar

1. Preheat the oven to 325°F.

2. In a small saucepan, combine the apple juice and dried apricots. Bring to a simmer over medium heat and then remove from the heat. Set aside to allow the apricots to rehydrate and puff up.

3. In a small cast-iron skillet over medium-high heat, heat the butter and olive oil. Add the celery, onion, garlic, parsley, and basil. Cook until the onion is translucent, about 8 minutes. Add the salt and pepper. In a large bowl, combine the onion mixture with the stuffing mix and Worcestershire sauce. Mix well and set aside to cool.

4. Prepare the loin for stuffing by cutting it nearly in half lengthwise (do not cut all the way through to the other side) and splaying it out flat like a book. Put a sheet of plastic wrap over the top and carefully pound the meat until it's ½ inch thick. Working from the center out, pound with an outward motion to get the meat thin enough but not so thin that it will tear apart. You need to be able to pick it up and handle it.

5. Drain and chop the apricots and add them to the stuffing mix. Now spread the stuffing mixture evenly onto the meat, leaving a border on the outside edges. Roll the meat up lengthwise. It will look like a pinwheel on the ends. Use kitchen twine to tie it at ½-inch intervals so that the filling does not fall out.

6. Put the loin on a rack in a shallow roasting pan. Cover the pan with foil—this will steam the loin and keep it moist. Bake for 50 minutes.

7. Uncover and bake until a meat thermometer inserted into the center reads 160°F, about 25 minutes longer. Remove from the oven and let stand for 10 minutes.

8. Meanwhile, in a small saucepan, combine the apricot preserves, balsamic, and brown sugar and heat over medium-low heat, stirring until smooth.

9. Remove the string from the loin and brush the meat with the apricot glaze. Cut the loin into pinwheel slices and serve drizzled with the remaining glaze.

Pork Chop CASSEROLE

Oh, my daddy loved a pork chop. He could eat them every night, so Mama would have to come up with ways to change 'em up. That's what this is; It's "Blake, I don't want pork chops but I'll figure out a way to change it up so you can have a pork chop." Soon enough Daddy wanted this recipe all the time.

SERVES 6

---

6 medium russet (baking) potatoes
Salt and black pepper
3 tablespoons unsalted butter
1 cup plus 1 tablespoon olive oil
1 pound button mushrooms, sliced
3 tablespoons all-purpose flour, plus more for dredging
1 cup heavy cream
6 boneless center-cut pork chops, each about ½ inch thick

---

1. Preheat the oven to 350°F. Grease a 9 × 13-inch baking dish.

2. Peel the potatoes and cut into round slices about ½ inch thick. Layer them in the bottom of the baking dish. Sprinkle with salt and pepper.

3. In a large skillet over medium-high heat, melt the butter with 1 tablespoon of the olive oil. Cook the mushrooms until golden brown, 8 to 10 minutes. Sprinkle with the 3 tablespoons flour and cook, stirring, to make a golden brown roux, about 5 minutes. Stir in the heavy cream and simmer until thickened, about 5 minutes longer.

4. In another large skillet over medium-high heat, heat the remaining 1 cup oil. Season the pork chops with salt and pepper and coat on both sides with flour, shaking off any excess. Fry the pork chops, in batches if necessary, until golden brown on each side, 6 to 8 minutes total.

5. Arrange the pork chops on top of the potatoes. Spoon the mushroom sauce over the pork chops and cover the dish with foil. Bake until the potatoes are fork tender, about 1 hour.

Sara's PORK CHOPS

I must say, one thing my daughter, Sarablake, can do is cook meat—sometimes better than me. So when it comes time to cook chops I give her a call. She has learned to cook at the apron strings of her Nana (my mama) and, just like me, she always puts her own spin on things. This is Sara's go-to recipe for tender, juicy, and sweet chops that she likes to serve with 'taters, mac and cheese, and applesauce—her three favorite vegetables. (Yes, mac and cheese and applesauce qualify as vegetables in Sara's book.)

SERVES 6

6 bone-in pork chops, each ¼ to ½ inch thick
2 tablespoons Montreal steak seasoning
Salt and black pepper
Buttermilk, for dredging
1½ cups self-rising flour (I use White Lily)
Peanut or vegetable oil, for deep-frying

1. Sprinkle the pork chops on both sides with Montreal steak seasoning and salt and pepper.

2. Dip the pork chops into the buttermilk, letting the excess drip off, then dredge each one in the flour. Allow the chops to rest on a large plate in the refrigerator for about 30 minutes.

3. Pour oil to a depth of 1 inch in a large, heavy skillet and heat over medium-high heat to 350°F. Test with a dash of flour—if the flour sizzles on contact, the oil is ready.

4. Once the oil is hot, and working in batches if necessary, slide the chops carefully into the pan and cook, turning once if they are not submerged in oil, until nicely browned, 8 to 10 minutes total.

Corned Beef HASH

I am fully Irish-American and I'm proud. We're determined and hardheaded, and we love good food. My family's roots lie in raising draft horses. That was a hard day's work, which meant a good, hearty, stick-to-your-ribs meal. Hash is just that, filling enough to help you get back out there and tend to the horses—which I have been told were just as hardheaded as my Irish ancestors who raised them.

SERVES 8

2 teaspoons vegetable oil
1 large onion, chopped
1 (16-ounce) bag frozen hash brown potatoes
3 pounds corned beef, chopped
½ cup low-sodium chicken broth
¼ cup chopped fresh parsley
Salt and black pepper

1. In a large cast-iron skillet over medium-high heat, heat the oil. Add the onion and cook until it starts to brown, 5 to 8 minutes. Add the potatoes and cook, stirring, until they brown in spots and become crusty, about 8 minutes more.

2. Stir in the corned beef and broth and cook, scraping up any browned bits, until the liquid is absorbed, 5 to 8 minutes. Add the parsley and season with salt and pepper to taste. Serve immediately.

Golden CUBE STEAKS

Cube steak is just that—meat that has been run through a "cuber," a machine that cuts crosshatches into the meat to break up the tendons and make tougher cuts, such as round steak, more tender (though just how tender depends on the quality of the meat to start with, of course). I ask the meat counter to cube my steaks right then and there so as not to get ones that have been sitting in the case a couple of days. This dish is one of those things we love to smother in gravy.

SERVES 4 TO 6

    1 large egg
    ½ cup whole milk
    2 tablespoons Worcestershire sauce
    1½ cups all-purpose flour
    1½ teaspoons Lawry's seasoned salt
    ½ teaspoon black pepper
    4 to 6 cube steaks (1¾ to 2½ pounds total)
    1 cup vegetable oil
    Simple Beef Gravy (recipe follows), for serving (optional)

1. In a medium bowl, whisk together the egg and milk. Stir in the Worcestershire sauce. In a shallow bowl using a fork to stir, mix the flour with the Lawry's and pepper.

2. Dip each of the steaks in the milk mixture, letting the excess drip off. Then dredge each steak in the seasoned flour, tapping off any excess.

3. In a cast-iron skillet over medium heat, heat the oil. Put the dredged steaks carefully into the hot oil; don't let it splash up and burn you. Fry until golden brown on both sides, about 3 minutes per side. Drain on paper towels.

4. Serve smothered with gravy, if desired.

SIMPLE BEEF GRAVY

This is great on cubed steak but I also spoon it on mashed potatoes and meatloaf—and believe it or not my husband likes it on cold, ripe cantaloupe in the morning. (He even got me hooked on it, too!)

MAKES ABOUT 1¾ CUPS

4 tablespoons unsalted butter
¼ cup self-rising flour
(I use White Lily)
1 cup milk
1 cup beef broth
Salt and pepper

1. In a cast-iron frying pan, melt the butter over medium-high heat. Stir in the flour and cook, stirring constantly, until lightly browned, 4 to 5 minutes.

2. In a measuring cup, combine the milk and beef broth. Pour half of the liquid into the pan. Stir until the mixture bubbles a little bit, about 3 minutes, then stir in the remaining liquid. Bring to a boil and stir continuously to keep it from sticking. Reduce the heat so that the mixture simmers gently. Cover the pan and simmer, stirring occasionally, until thickened, about 5 minutes.

3. Season with salt and pepper and serve hot.

Meatloaf TO STOP A MAN IN HIS TRACKS

If anyone tells you "you can't catch a man with food," well, they are *sooo* wrong. Food will catch a husband faster than all the bikinis in the world. It will also make your family happy. Pull this out of the oven and watch how it can make the kids put down the game controls and wash up for supper without a fight. Prepare a meatloaf and bring the family back to the table. I like to use 90% lean ground chuck bound with rolled oats, but to me it's that touch of whole-grain mustard that brings it all together. This meatloaf is not shy on flavor.

SERVES 6

2 pounds 90% lean ground chuck
2 large eggs
1 medium onion, finely chopped
1 tablespoon chopped fresh parsley
⅓ cup old-fashioned rolled oats
¼ cup mayonnaise (I use Duke's)
3 tablespoons ketchup
1 tablespoon whole-grain mustard
1 cup Italian-style bread crumbs
1 teaspoon salt
¼ teaspoon black pepper
Barbecue sauce, homemade (pages 65 and 66) or store-bought, for serving (optional)

1. Preheat the oven to 350°F.

2. In a large bowl, mix together the beef, eggs, onion, parsley, oats, mayonnaise, ketchup, mustard, bread crumbs, salt, and pepper (use your hands; they work best).

3. Shape the meat into a 5 × 12-inch loaf and put it on a rimmed baking sheet. Bake until the juices run clear, about 1 hour.

4. Serve slices topped with barbecue sauce, if you like.

Cheeseburger PIE

Yes, I put cheeseburgers in a pie shell. Well, my aunt Thelma did it first; I'm just carrying on the family tradition. I spent the first eleven years of my life on a mill hill, in Greenville, South Carolina, the textile capital of the world, where we still had soda jerks and mom-and-pop stores with in-house charge accounts. After school I would cook with my nana or grandma or hang out at my papa's store, listening to the old men tell fishing stories while drinking Coke out of glass bottles with peanuts in them. When those memories flood back, I think of the food we were making and this dish ranks right up there.

SERVES 8

PIE

1 unbaked 9-inch deep-dish pie crust, homemade (page 105) or store-bought (I use Pillsbury)
1 pound 90% lean ground beef
1 teaspoon salt
¼ teaspoon black pepper
½ teaspoon dried oregano
½ cup plain bread crumbs
½ cup tomato sauce
¼ cup chopped onion
¼ cup diced green bell pepper
1 teaspoon Montreal steak seasoning
½ teaspoon granulated garlic

TOPPING

1 large egg, lightly beaten
¼ cup whole milk
2 cups shredded sharp cheddar cheese (8 ounces)
½ teaspoon salt
½ teaspoon dry mustard
½ teaspoon Worcestershire sauce

1. Make the pie: Preheat the oven to 425°F.

2. Fit the pie dough into a 9-inch deep-dish pie pan and flute the edges.

3. In a medium skillet over medium heat, cook the meat, breaking it up with a wooden spoon, until browned, about 10 minutes.

4. Drain off the fat from the meat and discard. Stir in the salt, black pepper, oregano, bread crumbs, tomato sauce, onion, bell pepper, steak seasoning, and granulated garlic. Scoop the mixture into the pastry-lined pie pan. Press it down evenly in the pan.

5. Make the topping: In a medium bowl, combine the egg, milk, cheddar, salt, dry mustard, and Worcestershire sauce. Spread the topping over the filling.

6. Bake the pie until the cheese on top is bubbling and browned, about 30 minutes. Serve hot.

Hamburger STEW

Hamburger stew (or soup) has been around these parts forever. Here in the South we always make the best use of whatever we have on hand, and this is one of my go-to recipes when I need to clean out the canned goods in my pantry. As soon as it got a little chilly, Daddy would start asking for this stew. He's no longer with us, but when I make this it brings me closer to his memory. The good thing is it goes a long way, and after a couple of days you can use the leftovers in a casserole. It's just a plain old hearty, filling, good stew. And while there have been times when my pantry-purging recipes didn't work out, this is definitely not one of them.

SERVES 10 TO 12

```
3 pounds 90% lean ground beef
6 russet (baking) potatoes, diced
1 large onion, diced
2 (14.5-ounce) cans green beans, with liquid
2 (15.25-ounce) cans whole kernel corn, with liquid
1 (14.5-ounce) can sliced carrots, with liquid
1 (14.5-ounce) can stewed tomatoes
1 (15-ounce) can tomato sauce
2 (14.5-ounce) cans beef broth
3 tablespoons Montreal steak seasoning
```

1. In a large skillet over medium heat, cook the beef, breaking it up with a wooden spoon, until browned, about 10 minutes. Drain off the fat and discard.

2. Put the meat and remaining ingredients in a slow cooker and cook on medium for 4 hours. (Alternatively, cook in a large pot over low heat until the potatoes are tender, about 2 hours.)

Cheeseburger-without-the-Bun SOUP

Well, this is one of the easiest meals I've ever learned to make. My good friend Trudy whips it up for potlucks, and I always hope she will show up at our gatherings with her traveling slow cooker full so I can hover over it. When I make it, sometimes I leave the tomatoes out—dealer's choice. It's great on chips, as my kids like it, or just eaten with a spoon, like I do. It's not fancy, but oh boy is it warm and filling.

SERVES 10

1 pound 90% lean ground beef
10 slices bacon
2 pounds Velveeta, diced
2 pounds russet (baking) potatoes, peeled and shredded (use the large holes on a box grater)
1 (15-ounce) can chicken broth
1 (8-ounce) can RO*TEL tomatoes with chiles
Corn chips, for serving (optional)

1. In a large skillet over medium heat, cook the beef, breaking it up with a wooden spoon, until well browned, 10 to 12 minutes. Drain off and discard the fat.

2. In a nonstick skillet over medium heat, cook the bacon until crispy, 8 to 10 minutes. Drain on paper towels and then crumble the bacon.

3. Combine the beef, bacon, Velveeta, potatoes, broth, and tomatoes in a slow cooker and cook on low for 4 to 6 hours. Serve alone or with chips.

Beef CRUNCH BAKE

You could say this is a taco bake. It kind of is, but Mama—who would make this on family movie nights (this was back when Betamax came out, then VHS, and you could rent movies from a store)—called it a Beef Crunch Bake. She'd always get a chick flick and Daddy would sit and bear it with a smile because he loved my mama so much. And Mama would make this because she knew it made him and the whole family happy.

SERVES 12

1 pound 90% lean ground beef
1 medium onion, chopped
½ green bell pepper, chopped
8 ounces frozen corn kernels, thawed
1 tablespoon paprika
1 teaspoon chili powder
1 teaspoon garlic powder
1 teaspoon onion powder
½ teaspoon dried thyme
½ teaspoon sugar
1 cup salsa
1 (12-ounce) bag tortilla chips, crushed
2 cups shredded cheddar cheese (8 ounces)
Sour cream, for serving (optional)

1. Preheat the oven to 350°F. Grease a 9 × 13-inch baking dish.

2. In a large skillet over medium-high heat, brown the beef, onion, and bell pepper together, about 12 minutes. Stir in the corn, paprika, chili powder, garlic powder, onion powder, thyme, sugar, salsa, and ⅔ cup water, mixing well.

3. Spread half of the mixture on the bottom of the baking dish. Top with half of the chips and 1 cup of the cheddar. Add the remaining meat mix and top with the remaining chips and cheese.

4. Bake until the cheese is melted, about 20 minutes. Serve hot, with sour cream on the side, if desired.

Fried Liver WITH ONION GRAVY

We used to eat this dish every Tuesday night when I was growing up and I never liked it. But before you flip the page, you should know that I may owe my life to this dish. Fast-forward many years and I found myself eating it in the hospital while fighting cancer after extreme weight loss. At one point I weighed 561 pounds, but after an operation to help me lose weight, I went to the other end of the spectrum and dropped down to 72 pounds. I was starving, anemic, listless, dying—and eating this childhood food like it was going out of style to build myself back up. Well, the fried liver with onion gravy worked. I'm here, healthy, and sharing my former fear of this food to help you realize it's not so bad after all. In fact, you can still order it on menus all over the South and it still brings me back to my childhood.

SERVES 4

1 pound beef liver
½ cup self-rising flour (I use White Lily)
½ cup self-rising cornmeal
1 teaspoon salt
½ teaspoon black pepper (or to taste)
Peanut or vegetable oil, for frying
2 large onions, thinly sliced
½ cup beef broth

1. Rinse the liver with cold water and pat dry. If the pieces are large, cut them in half.

2. In a shallow dish, mix together the flour, cornmeal, salt, and pepper.

3. Pour oil to a depth of ½ to 1 inch in a heavy skillet (I use a cast-iron chicken fryer) and heat over high heat to about 365°F. Reduce heat to medium-high (about 325°F), add the onions, and cook, stirring frequently until they have browned lightly, about 10 minutes. Remove the onions from the pan and set aside on a plate.

4. Roll the liver pieces in the flour mixture. In the same skillet you used for the onions, cook the liver pieces in batches over medium to medium-high heat. Brown well on both sides, about 14 minutes total.

5. Once all the liver has been browned, return the onions and liver to the pan and pour in the beef broth. Reduce the heat to medium and cook until tender and cooked through, 3 to 5 minutes.

6. Transfer the liver to a serving platter, arranging the caramelized onions on top.

Squirrel POT PIE

Okay, I know I'm gonna catch it for this one, but I have to stick by who I am. We live off the land as much as possible, plant our own veggies and herbs, and yes, we do hunt and fish whenever time will allow. As odd as it may sound, I have noticed you can get rabbit and squirrel in the grocery stores here now. And this right here is a recipe that my great-granny made, and then my granny and daddy made, and then they taught me to make it. You can't get more authentic than that. And if you're wondering what squirrel tastes like, well, it tastes like chicken—pure white meat, yet pretty rich.

SERVES 6

6 squirrels, cleaned and quartered
1 teaspoon garlic powder
1 teaspoon ground cumin
1 teaspoon Italian seasoning
2 cups self-rising flour (I use White Lily), plus more for rolling the dough
1 large egg, lightly beaten
½ cup whole milk
Dash of salt
2 teaspoons black pepper
8 medium russet (baking) potatoes, peeled and diced
½ cup diced onion

1. Put the squirrels in a large pot and add enough cold water to cover. Add the garlic powder, cumin, and Italian seasoning. Bring the mixture to a boil and boil until the squirrel is tender, about 15 minutes. Remove the squirrel from the cooking broth, reserving the broth. When the squirrels are cool enough to handle, pull the meat from the bones and set aside.

2. In a bowl, combine the flour, egg, milk, salt, and pepper. Work into a dough and then into a small ball. On a lightly floured board, roll the dough out until it's ⅛ inch thick. Cut it into 3-inch squares.

3. Bring the reserved broth to a boil over high heat. Drop the dough squares, squirrel meat, potatoes, and onion into the boiling broth in layers until everything is in the pot. Cover the pot and cook over low heat at a low simmer until the potatoes are tender and the dough is cooked, 20 to 30 minutes.

Sunday Supper Pie,
page 104

SUNDAY SUPPERS

Fit for the preacher

Everybody knows you gotta know how to cook for the preacher—or the people in your life you really love. Those meals need to have a little more care and time given to them when compared with your usual weeknight rotation of dishes. Here are a few of my favorites; they're dressed to impress—and satisfy, too.

SOUTHERN FRIED CATFISH

MEATY STUFFED PEPPERS

Yankee Pot Roast, Southern Style

CHICKEN POT PIE

SHRIMP AND GRITS

Sunday Supper Pie

CRAB SOUFFLÉ

Southern FRIED CATFISH

Catfish is the only fish I eat. I know it's not the pick of the litter, but it's the fish for me. Living on the Gulf Coast of Florida half my life I had all the fresh seafood I could handle, but nonetheless I've always been drawn back to the firm, pure white meat of the catfish. Serve it up with a side of cheese grits and slaw and I'm right back at one of the day-long fish fries my parents used to host.

SERVES 6

¼ cup buttermilk
½ teaspoon cider vinegar
6 skinless catfish fillets (6 to 8 ounces each)
Peanut or vegetable oil, for deep-frying
3 tablespoons all-purpose flour
½ cup cornmeal
1 teaspoon paprika
1 teaspoon salt
½ teaspoon black pepper
½ teaspoon granulated garlic
½ teaspoon onion powder
½ teaspoon Old Bay seasoning
¼ teaspoon cayenne pepper

1. In a large bowl or rectangular baking dish, whisk together the buttermilk and cider vinegar. Add the fish fillets, turning to coat with the mixture. Let sit for 30 minutes to soften the fish.

2. Pour oil to a depth of 4 inches into a Dutch oven or deep pot and heat over medium-high heat to 350°F. Test with a dash of flour—if the flour sizzles on contact, the oil is ready.

3. Meanwhile, in a shallow pan, whisk together the flour, cornmeal, paprika, salt, black pepper, granulated garlic, onion powder, Old Bay, and cayenne.

4. Remove the fish one piece at a time from the buttermilk mixture and then coat both sides of the fillets in the flour mixture.

5. Fry the fish fillets in batches in the hot oil until golden brown, 3 to 4 minutes per side. Drain the fried fillets on paper towels. Serve hot.

Meaty STUFFED PEPPERS

What can I say about my Mark? Most people know he is my husband, but they may not know that he's also my biggest critic and he does not hold back. That's a good thing for coming up with new recipes. I go to him first because I know he's going to give me his thoughts straight up. When I came up with these beefy, pork-and-rice stuffed peppers he fell in love all over again (with my cooking).

SERVES 6

1½ cups long-grain white rice
6 medium bell peppers
½ pound 90% lean ground beef
½ pound ground pork
¼ cup hot water
1 cup diced tomato
1 medium onion, chopped
1 teaspoon salt
1 teaspoon garlic powder
1 teaspoon dry mustard
½ teaspoon black pepper
1 teaspoon basil paste (sold in a tube in the produce section)

1. Preheat the oven to 350°F.

2. Cook the rice according to the package directions.

3. Meanwhile, prepare the bell peppers by cutting around the stem on the top of each and removing the stem. Remove as many of the seeds as possible without cutting into the bottoms or sides of the peppers.

4. In a large skillet over medium-high heat, cook the beef and pork, breaking them up with a wooden spoon until browned, about 10 minutes. Add the hot water and simmer until the water evaporates, about 5 minutes. Add the tomato, onion, salt, garlic powder, dry mustard, black pepper, and basil paste and cook, stirring frequently, until the onion is soft, about 10 minutes.

5. Add the cooked rice to the meat mixture and stir to combine. Remove from the heat and stuff the peppers with the meat mixture.

6. Arrange the stuffed peppers in a baking pan that holds them snugly. Bake, uncovered, until the tops have browned, about 30 minutes.

Yankee Pot Roast,
SOUTHERN STYLE

Pot roast seems to be almost a lost art. It's something you never hear anyone talking about these days and yet I know it's still an after-church standard. To put a Southern spin on this Yankee dish, slap that hunk of meat in the slow cooker and add a cold beer. Now we're talking. Don't worry, the alcohol will cook off—you're just after the flavor.

SERVES 8

2 medium yellow onions, cut into eighths
6 russet (baking) potatoes, peeled
8 medium carrots, quartered
1 (3- to 4-pound) beef chuck pot roast
1 tablespoon Worcestershire sauce
1 teaspoon dried rosemary
½ teaspoon dried basil
½ teaspoon dried thyme
2 bay leaves
12 ounces beer, such as amber ale

1. In a slow cooker, combine the onions, potatoes, and carrots. Put the beef roast on top and then sprinkle the Worcestershire sauce, rosemary, basil, and thyme evenly over the roast. Put the 2 bay leaves on top of the roast. Pour the beer evenly over everything.

2. Cook on medium for 4 hours (or low for 8 hours, or high for 2 hours and 15 minutes) until the beef is fall-apart tender.

3. Discard the bay leaves, slice the pot roast, and serve with the vegetables.

Chicken POT PIE

Just about everyone has eaten a chicken pot pie at some point, but in my case the sheer volume was a bit overboard. When they came out premade, Mama must have fed them to us at least once a week. She was part of the TV-dinner generation and when those things were invented, she just about fell in love. Pull them out of the freezer, hardly any wait, and "ta da" supper was ready. Lord knows I love her and miss her every day—and I even catch myself saying, "I wonder if this is as good as Mama's frozen version"—but, truth be told, I know homemade is so much better.

SERVES 8

2 pounds boneless, skinless chicken breasts
2 cups chicken broth, plus more as needed
½ teaspoon salt
¼ teaspoon black pepper
1½ cups half-and-half
3 tablespoons unsalted butter
1 medium onion, chopped
1 cup chopped celery
⅓ cup all-purpose flour
1 tablespoon chopped fresh parsley
½ teaspoon dried thyme
1½ cups frozen mixed vegetables, thawed
2 medium russet (baking) potatoes, cut into ½-inch dice
2 unbaked 9-inch refrigerated pie crusts (I use store-bought for this recipe)
1 large egg, lightly beaten

1. In a large saucepan, combine the chicken breasts, chicken broth, salt, and pepper. Bring to a boil over medium-high heat and then reduce the heat to low. Cover and simmer until the chicken is cooked through, about 30 minutes. Remove the chicken from the broth, reserving the broth. When cool enough to handle, cut the chicken into pieces.

2. Pour the reserved chicken broth into a large bowl and spoon off any fat. Add enough canned broth to equal 1 cup, if needed. Pour in the half-and-half.

3. Preheat the oven to 400°F.

4. In the same saucepan over medium heat, melt the butter. Add the onion and celery. Cook, stirring, until tender, about 3 minutes. Stir in the flour until well blended. Gradually stir in the broth mixture, parsley, and thyme. Simmer, stirring constantly, until the sauce thickens and boils, about 5 minutes longer. Add the chicken, mixed vegetables, and potatoes to the pan and stir to combine.

5. Line a 9-inch deep-dish pie pan with one of the pie crusts. Pour in the chicken mixture, leaving enough space to put on the top crust. Cover the filling with the second pie crust, making sure to seal the edges by pinching together the top and bottom and then pressing against the lip of the dish. Cut a few vent holes in the top of the pastry and then brush the pastry with the beaten egg.

6. Bake until the crust is golden brown and the filling is bubbling, about 30 minutes. Let cool for 10 minutes and serve. The mixture will thicken while baking; have no fear.

Shrimp AND GRITS

Shrimp and grits is one of my favorite meals in the world. Given the choice, I would eat this dish over a prime rib. You see, I was raised for half of my life on Florida's Gulf Coast, where fresh shrimp are sweet and plentiful. And as much as I love those shrimp, the star of this rich and creamy dish really is the grits. We still have a working grits mill here in my hometown, and that's where I get mine.

SERVES 8

1 pound medium shrimp, peeled and deveined
1½ teaspoons Old Bay seasoning
¼ teaspoon salt
1 cup coarse-ground grits (such as stone-ground)
2 slices bacon, cut crosswise into thin strips
3 garlic cloves, sliced
3 cups heavy cream
1 (12-ounce) bag frozen corn kernels
1 cup freshly grated Parmesan cheese
3 green onions, sliced

1. In a medium bowl, toss the shrimp with the Old Bay.

2. In a large saucepan, bring 3 cups water and the salt to a boil. Gradually stir in the grits and reduce the heat to medium. Partially cover and cook, stirring occasionally, until thickened, about 10 minutes.

3. Meanwhile, in a large skillet over medium-high heat, cook the bacon until just crisp, about 6 minutes. Transfer the bacon to paper towels to drain.

4. Reduce the heat under the skillet to medium and add the garlic to the bacon fat in the pan. Cook the garlic until you can smell it, 30 seconds to 1 minute. Add the shrimp and cook, turning, until pink, about 3 minutes. Remove the shrimp and garlic to a bowl. Reserve the skillet.

5. In a medium saucepan over medium heat, heat 2 cups of the heavy cream. Add the corn and bring to a simmer. Cook until the corn is softened, about 10 minutes.

6. Stir the creamed corn into the cooked grits. Reduce the heat to medium-low, cover, and cook until well blended, about 5 minutes. Remove from the heat and let stand 5 minutes. Stir in the Parmesan.

7. Pour the remaining 1 cup heavy cream into the skillet over medium heat, scraping up any browned bits from the bottom of the pan. Simmer until slightly thickened, about 4 minutes. Stir in the shrimp and garlic and bacon pieces. Cook for 1 minute to heat through.

8. Pour the grits onto a platter. Top with the shrimp and cream sauce and garnish with the green onions.

Sunday Supper PIE

This is one from Mama. She would prep this butternut squash, potato, and beef pie and bake it once we got home from church. Back then, though we lived about nineteen miles south, we went to church in the town I live in now. By the time we got home it was already getting dark. This pie was in the oven while we had baths and got our school clothes ready for Monday morning.

SERVES 8

1 unbaked 9-inch pie crust, homemade (recipe follows)
or store-bought
1 medium butternut squash, peeled and diced (about 2 cups)
3 medium russet (baking) potatoes, peeled and diced
(about 2 cups)
5 tablespoons olive oil
1 teaspoon Lawry's seasoned salt
1 tablespoon dried thyme
1 pound beef, cut into ½-inch cubes (I use stew meat)
1 cup beef broth
2 tablespoons cornstarch
Salt and black pepper

1. Preheat the oven to 375°F.

2. Fit the pie dough into a 9-inch pie pan.

3. Arrange the squash and potatoes on a baking sheet. Drizzle with 2 tablespoons of the oil and sprinkle with the Lawry's and thyme. Toss to coat. Roast in the oven until tender, about 25 minutes.

4. Meanwhile, in a skillet over medium-high heat, heat the remaining 3 tablespoons oil. Add the beef pieces and brown well on all sides, about 8 minutes. Drain the beef on paper towels. Reserve the skillet.

5. Add the beef, squash, and potatoes to the pie shell.

6. Pour the beef broth into the pan juices in the skillet. Whisk in the cornstarch. Bring to a boil over high heat and whisk until thickened, about 4 minutes. Season with salt and pepper.

7. Pour the pan gravy over the meat and veggies. Bake until the crust is golden brown, about 25 minutes. Let cool for 10 minutes before cutting and serving.

HOMEMADE PIE CRUST

MAKES TWO 9-INCH PIE CRUSTS

2½ cups all-purpose flour,
plus more for rolling
the dough
1 teaspoon salt
2 tablespoons powdered sugar
12 tablespoons (1½ sticks)
very cold unsalted butter,
diced
½ cup shortening (I use
Crisco), well chilled
6 to 8 tablespoons ice water

1. In a large bowl, whisk together the flour, salt, and sugar to lighten them up. Cut the butter and shortening into the flour mixture, using a pastry blender or fork, until the pieces are about the size of butter beans. (You want larger pieces of fat in this crust.)

2. Add the ice water 1 tablespoon at a time until the dough comes together in a ball; do not overwork it. Divide it in half and cover each portion with plastic wrap. Refrigerate for at least 20 minutes.

3. Unwrap one of the pieces of dough. On a lightly floured surface, roll the dough out to fit a 9-inch pie pan (about 11 inches across for a deep dish and 10 inches for a regular pie pan). Fit it into the pan, trim and crimp the edges, and chill the pie shell for 10 minutes before filling. Repeat with the second piece of dough. (If you'd like, freeze them for future use. Wrap them airtight and freeze for up to 2 months.)

Crab SOUFFLÉ

While living on Florida's Gulf Coast as a child I fell in love with seafood. I'm not a big fish eater, but give me some shellfish, like crab, which I adore, and I'm happy as a clam. . . . This may not be everyone's cup of tea, but it is real good if you want to try a recipe that might be a little outside your comfort zone. Dive into a medium-textured (not too airy, not too firm) soufflé that's just chock-full of sweet buttery crabmeat.

SERVES 6

1 pound lump crabmeat
3 large egg whites
3 tablespoons unsalted butter
¼ cup all-purpose flour
1½ teaspoons salt
½ teaspoon dry mustard
1 cup whole milk
3 large egg yolks, beaten
2 tablespoons chopped fresh parsley
2 teaspoons grated onion
1 tablespoon fresh lemon juice

1. Pick through the crab and make sure there's no shell or cartilage left attached to the meat.

2. Preheat the oven to 350°F. Generously grease a 1½-quart baking dish (or six 8-ounce ramekins). Fill a baking pan big enough for the baking dish or ramekins to fit in with a couple inches of hot water.

3. Using an electric mixer, beat the egg whites until stiff.

4. In a medium saucepan over medium heat, melt the butter. Blend in the flour, salt, and dry mustard. Whisk in the milk gradually and whisk until thick and smooth, about 8 minutes.

5. Stir a little of the hot milk mixture into the egg yolks and then whisk the yolk mixture into the saucepan with the rest of the milk mixture. Once everything is combined, remove from the heat and stir in the parsley, onion, lemon juice, and crabmeat.

6. Fold in the egg whites. Scoop the mixture into the prepared baking dish and put the dish in the pan of hot water.

7. Bake until the soufflé is firm in the center, about 1 hour (or 30 minutes for ramekins). Do not open the oven during baking or the soufflé will fall. The soufflé should have a little jiggle in the middle. Serve immediately.

Daddy's Church Gathering
Chili, page 112

ENOUGH TO FEED a Crowd

Or the extra guests you weren't expecting . . .

What to do when you've got a big group of hunting and fishing buddies on their way over, or just a bunch of hungry young'uns? Here are my secrets for feeding a big crew with a bunch of stick-to-your-ribs, I-need-a-nap, I'm-so-full food. So hold on my fellow rednecks, we're gonna eat now. No fancy finger foods here—just good ol' fill-'er-up foods. Plus, these casseroles are perfect make-and-take foods to wow the potluckers in your town. You'll never again have to say, "I'll bring the cups and plates."

MEATBALLS FOR A CROWD

DADDY'S CHURCH GATHERING CHILI

Chicken Casserole

MAMA'S TUNA CASSEROLE

DADDYS CHICKEN AND RICE

Brunswick Stew

MOM-IN-LAW SKETTIE

HOLIDAY TURKEY

Holiday Whole Roast Ham

FAMILY FAVORITE HOLIDAY DRESSING

TACO SALAD: A MAIN MEAL

Meatballs FOR A CROWD

One thing we love are meatballs. We even like the frozen kind cooked in BBQ sauce or baked and covered in tomato sauce, but this is my family's favorite way to make them from scratch, with a little bit of cheese and a couple vegetables thrown into the mix.

MAKES ABOUT 75 MEATBALLS (SERVES 25 AS AN APPETIZER OR 12 AS A MAIN COURSE)

4 slices stale white bread
½ cup freshly grated Parmesan cheese
3 garlic cloves, minced
2 tablespoons chopped fresh parsley
1 small onion, finely diced
1 green bell pepper, finely diced
2 teaspoons coffee barbecue rub (I use Weber's), optional
Salt and black pepper
2 large eggs, lightly beaten
¼ cup whole milk
3 pounds 90% lean ground beef
2½ cups your favorite barbecue or spaghetti sauce

1. Tear the bread into very small pieces and put in a large bowl. Add the Parmesan, garlic, parsley, onion, bell pepper, barbecue rub (if using), and salt and black pepper to taste. Stir in the eggs and milk. Add the ground beef and mix with your hands, keeping the mixture well blended.

2. Preheat the broiler. Line a large rimmed baking sheet with foil.

3. Form the meat into 1-inch balls using a small cookie scoop and arrange on the prepared baking sheet, leaving space between the meatballs. Broil until just browned on the outside, 7 to 9 minutes.

4. Transfer the meatballs to a Dutch oven or deep pot, add the barbecue sauce, and bring to a simmer over medium heat. Simmer until cooked through and flavorful, about 20 minutes. (Alternatively, you can cook these in a slow cooker on medium for 2½ hours, or on low for 4 hours, or on high for 1½ hours.)

Daddy's CHURCH GATHERING CHILI

Okay, the first thing I have to say about this recipe is that my daddy always made the chili for all the big gatherings, no matter what the occasion. He was called on mainly because his chili was the best. I think it's the unexpected combination of spices that he put together that makes it so good, the shots of vinegar and dashes of celery salt and oregano. Daddy's recipe won me my second championship at the Saint George Island Chili Cook-off, and nowadays I'm the one to bring it to gatherings. I must warn you: This is not a small recipe. I tried to cut it in half but it just didn't taste the same. So get out your biggest pot and freeze half of this batch for later. Serve it up with sour cream, grated cheese, and saltines.

SERVES 25

8 pounds 90% lean ground beef or chuck
2 tablespoons unsalted butter
2 large red onions, chopped
4 jalapeño peppers, finely chopped
2 green bell peppers, diced
1 red bell pepper, diced
2 garlic cloves, chopped
1 (16-ounce) can Bush's Chili Beans (the one with the yellow label), with liquid
2 (30-ounce) cans dark red kidney beans, rinsed and drained
3 (14.5-ounce) cans stewed tomatoes
2 (14.5-ounce) cans diced tomatoes, drained
6 tablespoons distilled white vinegar
½ teaspoon hot sauce (I use Texas Pete)
3 tablespoons sugar
1 tablespoon chili powder
2 teaspoons ground cumin
1 teaspoon dried oregano
1 teaspoon celery salt
1 teaspoon Lawry's seasoned salt
1 teaspoon salt
⅛ teaspoon cayenne pepper
1 tablespoon ground cinnamon (optional)
Sour cream, grated cheese, and saltines, for serving

1. In a very large pot over medium-high heat, cook the ground beef, breaking it up with a wooden spoon, until browned, about 12 minutes. Drain the fat from the pan and set the meat aside.

2. Melt the butter in the pot over medium heat. Add the onions, jalapeños, green and red bell peppers, and garlic and cook until softened, 8 to 10 minutes.

3. Return the beef to the pot and stir in the chili beans, kidney beans, stewed and diced tomatoes, vinegar, hot sauce, sugar, chili powder, cumin, oregano, all three salts, and the cayenne. Make sure everything is mixed well.

4. Reduce the heat so that the chili simmers and cook for about 4 hours so that the flavors will blend completely. It's got to simmer that long with all the seasonings to be good. At this point, add the ground cinnamon, if you'd like. (Daddy didn't add cinnamon but I like the way it makes the chili wake up.)

5. Serve right away with sour cream, grated cheese, and saltines or let cool and then cover and refrigerate overnight (it's even better reheated the next day) or freeze for up to a month.

Chicken CASSEROLE

Nobody is going to get too excited about a casserole, I know. But you are going to love a good one-pot dish you can travel with, freeze for later, have on hand for the hubby to bake when you have a night off, or pull together when company is coming and you have to fix something to feed a group. I've got ya covered right here.

SERVES 12

1 (16-ounce) box bow-tie pasta
Cooking spray
3 to 4 cups chopped cooked chicken (I use rotisserie chicken)
1 (12-ounce) package frozen broccoli florets
1½ cups Homemade Cream of Chicken Soup (page 38)
¾ cup mayonnaise (I use Duke's)
1 teaspoon fresh lemon juice
½ teaspoon salt
¼ teaspoon black pepper
1½ cups shredded cheddar cheese (6 ounces)
Butter crackers, crumbled (about 1 sleeve, enough to cover the top of the casserole)

1. Cook the pasta according to the package directions until just underdone. Drain well.

2. Coat a 3-quart baking dish with cooking spray.

3. In a large bowl, stir together the chicken, broccoli, and pasta.

4. In another bowl, combine the soup, mayonnaise, lemon juice, salt, pepper, and half of the cheddar. Mix well.

5. Pour the soup mixture over the chicken and stir well. Pour into the prepared baking dish. Sprinkle the butter crackers on top and then sprinkle with the remaining cheddar.

6. Bake until the cheese is bubbling, 40 to 45 minutes. Let sit for 10 minutes before serving.

Mama's TUNA CASSEROLE

Nothing brings back my childhood faster than Mama's tuna casserole—which was the only way she could get me to eat tuna. That is until I grew up and realized that I really do like tuna! I sometimes add bread crumbs to the top of this for a little extra crunch.

SERVES 12

1 (16-ounce) package egg noodles
1 cup mayonnaise (I use Duke's)
2 cups Cream of Celery Soup (page 148)
1½ cups evaporated milk
2 cups grated cheddar cheese (8 ounces)
1 cup chopped celery
1 small onion, finely chopped
1 (4-ounce) jar pimentos, drained
8 ounces button mushrooms, sliced
2 (5-ounce) cans water-packed tuna, with the liquid
2 teaspoons black pepper

1. Cook the egg noodles according to the package directions until just underdone. Drain well.

2. Preheat the oven to 325°F. Grease a 10 × 15-inch baking dish.

3. In a large bowl, mix together the mayonnaise, soup, evaporated milk, 1½ cups of the cheddar, the celery, onion, pimentos, mushrooms, tuna and liquid, and pepper. Stir in the egg noodles.

4. Spoon the mixture into the baking dish. Sprinkle the remaining ½ cup cheddar on top.

5. Bake until the casserole doesn't jiggle when you nudge the dish, about 30 minutes.

Daddy's CHICKEN AND RICE

My daddy loved to be in the kitchen, and chicken and rice was one of his best meals. There's nothing that has quite such a big and bold meaty chicken flavor as this recipe. It's chicken on steroids (in a really good way).

SERVES 8

3 pounds bone-in, skinless chicken breast halves
1 medium onion, diced
2 celery stalks, diced
2 medium carrots, diced
2 chicken bouillon cubes
10 tablespoons (1¼ sticks) unsalted butter
1½ cups long-grain white rice
1 tablespoon olive oil
1 pound cremini or white button mushrooms, sliced
1¼ cups Homemade Cream of Chicken Soup (page 38)

1. Put the chicken in a 2-quart Dutch oven. Add enough water to cover and bring to a boil. Add the onion, celery, carrots, bouillon cubes, and 4 tablespoons of the butter. Reduce the heat and let the mixture simmer until the chicken is cooked through, about 20 minutes. The water will have reduced by about half.

2. Remove the chicken and set it aside to cool. Scoop out and set aside 1 cup of the broth.

3. Add the rice to the broth and vegetables in the pot, stir once, and cover the pot. Return the pot to medium heat and bring the liquid to a simmer (not a boil). Cook until the rice is tender, about 25 minutes.

4. Meanwhile, in a skillet over medium-high heat, melt 2 tablespoons of the butter with the olive oil. Add the mushrooms and cook until browned, about 10 minutes (they will reduce in size by half).

5. Add the mushrooms, cream of chicken soup, and remaining 4 tablespoons butter to the rice. Stir in the reserved cup of broth.

6. Pull the meat off of the chicken bones, shred it, and then add it to the pot. Let the mixture simmer until the rice is softened up, creating a creamy texture, about 20 minutes. Fluff with a fork and serve.

Brunswick STEW

I'm not sure if this is purely Southern, or if we just claim it, or if we just claim to do it best, but this is one of the things I go for when it gets cold. Brunswick stew was a dish I didn't like as a kid, but my taste buds have grown up and now we even take it on winter picnics to the mountains, complete with cornbread. This is a rich, rib-sticking, spicy, filling stew.

SERVES 20

2 tablespoons olive oil
1 tablespoon unsalted butter
2 medium onions, diced
3 garlic cloves, chopped
1 pound shredded cooked pork
1 pound shredded cooked chicken or turkey
1 (12-ounce) bag frozen corn
3 medium russet (baking) potatoes, peeled and diced
1 (28-ounce) can diced or stewed tomatoes
1½ cups ketchup
½ cup barbecue sauce, homemade (pages 65 and 66) or store-bought
5 tablespoons Worcestershire sauce
1 tablespoon cider vinegar
1 tablespoon red pepper flakes
2 bay leaves
½ teaspoon dry mustard

1. In a Dutch oven over medium heat, heat the olive oil and butter. Add the onions and garlic and cook until the onions soften and are almost translucent, about 4 minutes.

2. Stovetop version: Stir in the remaining ingredients and cook, stirring often, over medium heat for 1 hour. Reduce the heat to low and simmer until the stew is thick and the meat is very tender, 3 to 4 hours.

Slow-cooker version: Transfer the onion mixture to a slow cooker and add the remaining ingredients. Set the slow cooker to high for 1 hour. Reduce to low and cook until the stew is thick and the meat is very tender, 4 to 6 hours.

3. Discard the bay leaves before serving.

Mom-in-Law SKETTIE

It wasn't 'til I married my husband that I got to try my mother-in-law's "skettie." I could eat spaghetti every day and not get tired of it—but hers? I could eat it three times a day and still ask for more. It's just that good. Like a lot of family standbys, there's not really a recipe that she follows. This is what she has shown me while she makes it in the kitchen. Over the past few years I have adapted my own version that's pretty darn good.

This recipe makes a bunch of food fit for a crowd. But go ahead and make it for just your family and you'll be sure to have plenty for the next day. I try to make it on Fridays so that the whole family has it to eat through the weekend—plus, it's even better the day after.

SERVES 15

3 pounds 80% lean ground chuck
2 (15-ounce) cans tomato sauce
1 (28-ounce) can diced tomatoes
1 (6-ounce) can tomato paste
2 tablespoons dried basil
2 tablespoons dried oregano
2 bay leaves
2 garlic cloves, minced
3 tablespoons sugar
Salt and black pepper
2 (1-pound) package spaghetti

1. In a large Dutch oven over medium heat, cook the ground chuck, breaking it up with a wooden spoon, until browned, about 16 minutes. Drain off the fat and discard.

2. In the same pot, stir together the tomato sauce, diced tomatoes with their juices, tomato paste, basil, oregano, bay leaves, garlic, sugar, and salt and pepper to taste.

3. Simmer over low heat for at least 3 hours. (Alternatively, cook in a slow cooker on medium for 4 hours, or on low for 8 hours, or on high for 2 hours.)

4. Cook the pasta according to the package directions. Drain well.

5. Take out the bay leaves before you serve the meat sauce over the pasta.

Holiday TURKEY

What you see before you is my well-guarded Thanksgiving recipe. It may seem like a lot of steps, but it isn't, really, and always makes a juicy (never dry) bird that's as flavorful as can be.

SERVES 8 TO 12

Cooking spray
1 tablespoon all-purpose flour
1 (12- to 18-pound) whole turkey, thawed if frozen
8 tablespoons (1 stick) unsalted butter, cut into pats
1 teaspoon dried thyme
1 teaspoon dried rosemary
1 teaspoon Lawry's seasoned salt
1 tablespoon dried sage
½ teaspoon flaky sea salt
⅛ teaspoon black pepper
2 medium carrots, peeled and cut into 2-inch chunks
2 celery stalks, halved
1 medium onion, peeled and halved
4 garlic cloves, peeled

1. Preheat the oven to 350°F. Coat the inside of a turkey-size (for 8 to 24 pounds) oven cooking bag (I use Reynolds) with cooking spray. Put the flour in the bag and shake to coat the interior.

2. Remove the neck and giblets from the cavity of the turkey. Rinse the turkey under cold water and pat dry with paper towels. Insert the pats of butter underneath the skin of the turkey—breasts, legs, and thighs.

3. In a small bowl, stir together the thyme, rosemary, Lawry's, sage, sea salt, and pepper. Sprinkle and rub the herb mixture over the turkey, turning to coat the bottom as well as inside the cavity of the bird.

4. Put the turkey inside the oven bag. Add the carrots, celery, onion, and garlic to the bird cavity. Close the oven bag with a nylon tie, then cut four ½-inch slits into the top of the cooking bag. Put the turkey in the bag in a roasting pan. Tuck the ends of the bag into the pan.

5. Roast the turkey until cooked through, 3 to 3½ hours. There is no need to baste because the bag will keep the turkey moist. Let rest for 20 minutes before carving and serving.

Holiday WHOLE ROAST HAM

As I have always said, I have a real love for Coca-Cola. It's been a childhood treat since my grandpa would pour a few peanuts into the bottle. So one day while sitting in my kitchen and sipping a cool one, I thought, "If I can use it in cake and chicken, then why not ham?" The trick is to use bone-in ham. Don't be shy. Just get that big ham; the bone adds such good flavor.

SERVES 8 TO 10

1 (8- to 10-pound) bone-in ham
1 (15.25-ounce) can juice-packed pineapple rings, juices reserved
½ cup honey
1 cup packed light brown sugar
1 (8-ounce) jar maraschino cherries, juices reserved
1 (12-ounce) can Coca-Cola (not diet)

1. Preheat the oven to 375°F.

2. Put the ham in a large roasting pan. Using a sharp paring knife, score the skin ½ inch deep in two sets of opposing diagonal lines to create diamond shapes on the surface. Bake the ham, uncovered, until nicely browned, about 2 hours.

3. Meanwhile, in a medium saucepan, stir together the pineapple juice (about ½ cup) with the honey, brown sugar, cherry juice from the jar, and the Coke. Simmer, stirring, until it thickens a bit, 3 to 4 minutes. Remove from the heat.

4. Using a brush, coat the ham completely with the glaze, making sure to coat inside the diamonds and the sides. Attach the pineapple slices to the outside of the ham, securing them with toothpicks, then stick a cherry in the middle of each ring.

5. Continue baking until the ham is deeply browned all over, 40 to 50 minutes longer. Let cool for 20 minutes or more before thinly slicing.

Family Favorite
HOLIDAY DRESSING

Oh, the things I do for y'all, like spilling all my well-guarded family recipes just because I love writing cookbooks and sharing a love of food with y'all. The combination of homemade and Jiffy cornbreads with herbed stuffing is killer. Another secret: We don't always wait for the holidays for this dressing (not stuffing—I bake it alongside the turkey, not inside). I make a big batch and then freeze it so that we can have dressing any time of year.

SERVES 20

1½ cups cornmeal
¾ cup all-purpose flour
3 tablespoons sugar
1½ teaspoons baking powder
Salt and black pepper
2 large eggs
½ cup buttermilk
¼ cup vegetable oil
2 (8.5-ounce) boxes Jiffy corn muffin mix
2 tablespoons unsalted butter
4 slices bacon, chopped
1 medium onion, diced
4 celery stalks, chopped
1 green bell pepper, diced
4 large eggs, hard-boiled, peeled, and chopped
1 (15-ounce) bag herbed bread stuffing mix
1½ tablespoons ground sage, or 3 tablespoons chopped fresh
2 tablespoons Montreal steak seasoning
4 cups chicken broth
2½ cups Cream of Celery Soup (page 148)

1. Preheat the oven to 400°F. Put a 10-inch cast-iron skillet in the oven to warm.

2. In a large bowl, mix together the cornmeal, flour, sugar, baking powder, a ¼ teaspoon salt, the eggs, buttermilk, and oil until smooth. Pour the mixture into the hot cast-iron pan. Bake until golden brown around the edges and a toothpick inserted in the center comes out clean, about 30 minutes. Set aside to cool.

3. Bake the Jiffy mix according to the directions on the box for cornbread. Cool completely.

4. Preheat the oven to 350°F. Grease a 10 × 15-inch baking dish.

5. In a skillet over medium-high heat, melt the butter and cook the bacon until crisp, 6 to 9 minutes. Add the onion, celery, and bell pepper and cook until tender, about 4 minutes.

6. Crumble both the homemade and Jiffy cornbreads into the prepared baking dish. Scrape the vegetables in there, too. Stir in the hard-boiled eggs, stuffing mix, sage, steak seasoning, chicken broth, and celery soup. Mix well using your hands. Season with salt and black pepper.

7. Bake until the center is set and doesn't jiggle when you tap the pan, about 45 minutes. Serve hot. Leftovers keep well in the freezer. Reheat in the oven before serving.

Taco Salad: A MAIN MEAL

My daughter asks for this dish at least once a week. Mama made it the whole time I was growing up, and over the years we have changed it up. Before you gasp while you read the ingredients here, just sit down and grab a glass of tea and catch your breath. I know Thousand Island dressing is not something you would normally put in this kind of salad, but believe me it works. I pride myself on my ability to think outside the box and be fearless with food. But I always say recipes are just a guide; if y'all don't like Thousand Island, then try ranch or salsa and make it your own. When you need to feed 'em fast, this comes together quick, and it's filling.

SERVES 12

2 pounds 90% lean ground beef
⅓ cup Taco Seasoning (recipe follows)
1 head iceberg lettuce, cut into bite-size pieces
4 cups shredded cheddar cheese (16 ounces)
1 (12-ounce) bag Doritos
1 (14-ounce) bag white corn tortilla chips
Thousand Island Dressing (recipe follows)
1 tomato, diced

1. In a skillet over medium-high heat, cook the beef, breaking it up with a wooden spoon, until browned and cooked through, 10 to 15 minutes. Drain off the fat and discard; put the meat in a bowl.

2. In a small bowl, stir together the taco seasoning and ¼ cup warm water. Pour over the browned meat and mix well.

3. Put the lettuce in a large serving bowl. Add the cheddar and stir well. Crunch up both bags of chips into small pieces and add to the serving bowl.

4. Spoon the seasoned meat over the lettuce mixture and stir until blended. Add the dressing to taste (I use all of it) and mix well. Sprinkle the diced tomato on top. Serve warm.

TACO SEASONING

3 tablespoons chili powder
3 tablespoons ground cumin
2 tablespoons salt
2 tablespoons black pepper
1 tablespoon paprika
1½ teaspoons garlic powder
1½ teaspoons onion powder
1½ teaspoons dried oregano

Combine all of the ingredients in a jar with a lid. Store in a cool dry place. Use as needed.

THOUSAND ISLAND DRESSING

2 cups mayonnaise
(I use Duke's)
¼ cup ketchup
2 tablespoons sweet pickle relish
1 tablespoon finely minced onion
1 teaspoon fresh lemon juice
2 teaspoons sugar
Pinch each of salt and black pepper

In a medium bowl, combine all of the ingredients. Refrigerate in a sealed container for up to several weeks.

SIDES, 'TATERS & 'Maters

And other things you grow to eat

One of the great things about where we live is our long growing season. We have the perfect weather to get fresh veggies most of the year. That said, we still have things that are around for only a short time, and we make the most of them when they crop up. I hope this chapter will make you want to dig in the dirt and plant some veggies. Not only is it cheaper to grow your own, but it also keeps you on your toes in the inspiration department; you never know what's going to crop up exactly when, but when it does, you have to figure out how to cook it for supper!

CORN FRITTERS

CREAMED CORN

Corn Pudding

BEANS COOKED WITH HAM HOCKS

GREEN BEANS FROM NANA'S KITCHEN

Daddy's Squash Bake

ROASTED CROOKED YELLOW SQUASH

BROCCOLI CASSEROLE

Real Southern Collards

PUMPKIN CURRY SOUP

CREAM OF CELERY SOUP

Cream of Mushroom Soup

SWEET 'TATER SOUFFLÉ

MASHED 'TATERS

Rice and Gravy

FRIED GREEN 'MATERS

FRIED OKRA

Fried Cabbage

CHEESE GRITS FROM THE FLORIDA COAST

Corn FRITTERS

As you can tell, I love me some corn. These corn balls are little kisses of amazing. You can even drizzle them with a bit of pancake syrup and they go up about ten levels of good. That's how my husband loves 'em.

MAKES ABOUT 20 FRITTERS (SERVES 8 TO 10)

```
4 ears corn, husked
1 cup all-purpose flour
1 teaspoon baking powder
½ teaspoon salt
½ cup buttermilk
Peanut or vegetable oil, for deep-frying
```

1. Cut the kernels off the cobs into a bowl.

2. In a medium bowl, stir together the flour, baking powder, and salt. Stir in the buttermilk and corn and mix well.

3. Pour oil to a depth of 2 inches in a heavy-bottomed pot and heat over medium-high heat to 325°F.

4. Working in batches, drop the batter by the spoonful into the hot oil. Be sure to turn the fritters so they don't burn. Cook until golden brown, about 5 minutes. Drain on paper towels and serve warm.

MY GARDEN

I've always got a little patch growing in the backyard where we harvest cukes, corn, bell peppers, onions, potatoes, butter lettuce, squash, watermelons, eggplant . . . and then whatever else strikes my fancy at the feed and seed store that year. We grow the Big Boy tomatoes in front of the house so that we can tie them to the banisters as they get taller. I also keep a little herb garden where I grow basil, lemon basil, thyme, lavender, rosemary, cilantro, oregano, mint (a sweet tea essential), and a few types of peppers.

Creamed CORN

Creamed corn is one of the things we Southerners find ourselves waiting for all year. When the summer hits and the corn comes in it's one of our go-to recipes. You either love or hate creamed corn. While I don't like canned cream corn, homemade? I'm all over it. This recipe is the one Nana used, and I still make it the same way to this day.

SERVES 12

8 ears corn, husked
4 tablespoons (½ stick) unsalted butter
3 tablespoons fresh bacon drippings
1 teaspoon sugar
1 tablespoon all-purpose flour
½ teaspoon salt
½ teaspoon black pepper
1 (12-ounce) can evaporated milk

1. Cut the kernels off the cobs into a bowl. Then scrape the cobs with the back of a table knife to get all of the milk and pulp into the bowl.

2. In a large deep pan over medium-high heat, melt the butter with the bacon grease. Stir in the corn and its juices, 3 tablespoons water, and the sugar. Cook until the corn is tender, about 20 minutes.

3. Stir together the flour with 1 table-spoon water until blended. Stir into the corn and add the salt and pepper. Gradually add the evaporated milk, stirring constantly. Simmer over low heat for about 10 minutes longer. Do not let boil. Serve hot.

Corn PUDDING

I learned how to make this Sunday side dish at Granny's apron strings. It's how she made this Southern classic until she got up in years—then it was my turn. It's good enough to pass on to y'all.

SERVES 8

½ cup self-rising flour (I use White Lily)
2 tablespoons sugar
3 cups frozen or fresh corn kernels (from about 6 ears)
¼ cup sliced green onions
¼ cup chopped red bell pepper
3 large eggs
1 cup heavy cream
4 tablespoons (½ stick) unsalted butter, melted
Salt and black pepper

1. Preheat the oven to 350°F. Grease a 9-inch square baking dish.

2. In a small bowl, combine the flour and sugar. In another bowl, combine the corn, green onions, and bell pepper.

3. In a large bowl, whisk together the eggs, heavy cream, and melted butter. Gradually add the flour mixture and whisk until smooth. Stir in the corn mixture and season with salt and black pepper to taste.

4. Pour into the prepared baking dish and bake for 25 to 30 minutes. Remove from the oven and stir gently with a long-pronged fork. Return to the oven and continue cooking until set and browned, 25 to 30 minutes longer. Remove from the oven and allow to sit for 10 minutes before serving.

Beans COOKED WITH HAM HOCKS

Daddy would always threaten me with, "If you and your mama don't stop shopping, we're gonna be living on beans and rice." With beans like these, full of smoky flavor from the ham hocks, I might not mind so much. Add a little side of Corn Pudding (page 137) and you've got a proper, quick meal. This may seem like a lot of beans when you start cooking, but don't worry: They cook down by half.

SERVES 8

1 pound dried pinto beans (or another dried bean of your choice, such as navy or Great Northern, or lima beans)

1 large onion, chopped

3 good-size smoked ham hocks (or 8 ounces ham steak, diced)

1 teaspoon liquid smoke flavoring (optional)

Salt and black pepper

1. Sort through the beans for any of the dirt or rocks that sometimes find their way into a bag of beans. Rinse the beans, put them in a large bowl, and cover with a couple inches of cold water. Soak the beans overnight.

2. Drain the beans and put them in your slow cooker. Add 5 cups water, the onion, ham hocks, and liquid smoke (if using). Cook on medium for 3 hours (or on low for 6 hours, or high for 1½ hours).

3. Season with salt and pepper. Turn down to low and cook until the beans are tender and the meat falls off the bone, up to 30 minutes more. Check the level of water every 30 minutes during this time. If the beans start to get a little dry, add hot water, 1 cup at a time.

4. Discard the bones and serve the beans with the pieces of ham hock.

Green Beans
FROM NANA'S KITCHEN

The smell of green beans cooking always reminds me of Nana's house. She made them every Sunday for dinner along with fried chicken. Hers were the best—I think because she had bacon grease on standby, always. Even now I save up my bacon grease in a mason jar to use as needed. If you want to bulk up this side dish a bit you can add little 'taters to the beans.

SERVES 12

3 tablespoons unsalted butter

¼ cup fresh bacon drippings

2 pounds green beans, cut into 1-inch pieces

2 (12-ounce) cans small whole white potatoes (optional, but I like 'em)

Salt and black pepper

Bring a large pot of salted water to a boil. Add the butter, bacon grease, beans, and potatoes (if using). Boil until the beans are just tender or to your liking, 8 to 12 minutes. Drain well. Season with salt and pepper and serve.

Daddy's SQUASH BAKE

Daddy was a big fan of squash and so am I. We grow our own fresh squash and the pleasure they give me when I cook with them is right up there with picking a fresh tomato off the vine and eating it with a little salt. Summer always brings a bumper crop. This is a hide-the-veggies-and-the-kids-will-eat-them kind of dish that's creamy with a crunchy browned topping.

SERVES 12

```
4 medium yellow squash
8 tablespoons (1 stick) unsalted butter, melted
1½ cups Homemade Cream of Chicken Soup (page 38)
1 medium onion, chopped
1 large egg, lightly beaten
Salt and black pepper
2 cups crumbled stale cornbread or plain bread crumbs
```

1. Preheat the oven to 350°F.

2. In a Dutch oven or ovenproof pot, bring water to a boil—enough to cover the squash. Add the whole squash and boil until tender, about 10 minutes. Drain the water, leaving the squash in the pot.

3. Add the butter, soup, onion, and egg and season with salt and pepper. Stir well. Sprinkle the crumbs over the top.

4. Bake until golden brown on top, 30 to 40 minutes.

Roasted CROOKED YELLOW SQUASH

Yellow squash is everywhere in the summer and often keeps going through much of the fall. You can do so much with them—which is good, because we harvest so many crooknecks over the course of a season! This is the way my family loves them best—simple and good.

SERVES 8

4 tablespoons (½ stick) unsalted butter
1 medium onion, sliced
2 garlic cloves, crushed
1 teaspoon dried thyme
½ teaspoon dried rosemary
3 pounds yellow squash (about 6 medium), sliced lengthwise
Salt and black pepper

1. Preheat the oven to 350°F.

2. Put the butter in a 9 × 13-inch baking dish and stick it in the oven to melt.

3. Add the onion, garlic, thyme, rosemary, and squash to the dish and season with salt and pepper. Bake until tender, about 30 minutes. Serve hot.

Broccoli CASSEROLE

This creamy, cheesy dish is a standard in our house. We serve it every holiday, for sure, and for every family potluck. It was the only way Mama could get me to eat broccoli when I was growing up. I wasn't crazy about it then, but now I love it any way it comes.

SERVES 12

Cooking spray
4 cups fresh broccoli florets, or 2 (12-ounce) packages frozen chopped broccoli
1 cup mayonnaise (I use Duke's)
1 cup shredded sharp cheddar cheese (4 ounces)
2 cups Cream of Mushroom Soup (page 149)
2 large eggs, lightly beaten
Salt and black pepper
2½ cups crushed Ritz crackers
3 tablespoons unsalted butter, melted

1. Preheat the oven to 350°F. Coat a 9 × 13-inch baking dish with cooking spray.

2. In a pot fitted with a steamer basket, bring 1 to 2 inches of water to a boil over high heat. Steam the broccoli in the basket, covered, until tender, about 8 minutes for fresh or 12 minutes for frozen.

3. In a large bowl, combine the broccoli, mayonnaise, cheddar, soup, and eggs. Season with salt and pepper and mix well. Spoon the mixture into the prepared baking dish. Top with the crushed crackers and pour the melted butter evenly over the crackers.

4. Bake until set and browned on top, about 35 minutes.

Real Southern COLLARDS

Collards ought to be the one thing that everyone is required by law to know how to make if you have any state in the South listed on your birth certificate or you move below the Mason-Dixon line. They are so underappreciated and yet are a truly wonderful vegetable. I hope you enjoy the way that I was taught to make them. That is to say, may you hear angels singing as you eat them—sprinkled with vinegar or pepper sauce, of course.

SERVES 8 TO 10

½ pound fatback, sliced (optional)
½ pound smoked hog jowl, cut into chunks
2 tablespoons distilled white vinegar
¼ cup sugar
2 large bunches collard greens, center ribs removed, leaves coarsely chopped
Salt and black pepper
Pepper sauce or more distilled white vinegar, for serving

1. In a 6-quart Dutch oven over medium heat, cook the fatback (if using) and hog jowl until crisp, 8 to 10 minutes. Remove the fatback and jowl from the pot and set aside on a plate. Reserve one quarter of the drippings in the pot.

2. Pour 4 cups water into the pot with the drippings, add the white vinegar and sugar, and bring to a boil. Add one third of the greens to the pot and cook, stirring frequently until wilted, about 2 to 3 minutes. Fish out the greens and put on a big plate. Repeat twice using the remaining greens.

3. Return all the greens, the fatback, and jowl to the pot and reduce the heat to low. Add 1 cup water and simmer very gently, stirring once or twice, until the collards are tender, about 2 hours.

4. Season with salt and black pepper. Serve ladlefuls of the greens with hot sauce or vinegar for sprinkling on top.

Pumpkin Curry SOUP

Before we got married, Mark had never had anything with curry in it, and he had never had pumpkin soup, either. Now he begs for this soup. I made it on a television show once and the producer, my friend Jamarcus Gatson, always asks me, "When are you gonna make my soup for me again?" Needless to say, this is one of those recipes that you try once and then find yourself making on demand, over and over.

SERVES 6

8 tablespoons (1 stick) unsalted butter
1 medium onion, chopped
2 garlic cloves, minced
3 tablespoons curry powder
1 tablespoon ground coriander
Salt and black pepper
3 cups chicken broth
2 (15-ounce) cans unsweetened pumpkin puree (not pumpkin pie mix)
1 cup heavy cream
Roasted pumpkin seeds, for serving (optional)

1. In a medium pot over medium heat, melt the butter. Add the onion and garlic and cook until the onion is translucent, about 8 minutes. Stir in the curry powder, coriander, and salt and pepper to taste.

2. Add the chicken broth, pumpkin, and ½ cup cream and stir until blended. Reduce the heat and simmer until thickened, about 20 minutes.

3. Whip the remaining ½ cup heavy cream and serve the soup with a dollop of cream on top and pumpkin seeds, if desired.

Cream of Celery SOUP

Skip that canned soup and make it homemade! The trick is to let it cool down and then pour it into freezer bags in 1½-cup servings. You can then substitute it for the can of soup in a recipe or thaw it out on a cold night and pair it with a grilled cheese sandwich for a warm-you-up meal.

MAKES 6 CUPS (SERVES 6)

4 tablespoons (½ stick) unsalted butter
5 cups finely diced celery, including leaves
1 large onion, finely diced
3 garlic cloves, minced
2 quarts chicken broth
2 tablespoons dried tarragon
1 cup buttermilk
1 cup heavy cream
Salt and black pepper

1. In a large, heavy saucepan over medium-high heat, melt the butter. Add the celery and onion and cook until soft, about 8 minutes. Add the garlic and cook until golden, 2 to 3 minutes.

2. Pour in the broth and increase the heat to high to bring to a boil. Add the tarragon, reduce the heat to low, and add the buttermilk and cream. Simmer until thickened, about 20 minutes.

3. Using an immersion blender (or in batches in a stand blender), blend until smooth. Taste and season with salt and pepper. I often wait for the soup to cool and then freeze it for later use.

Cream of *Mushroom* SOUP

Creamed soups are something we swear by in the South. They can be stirred into just about everything, and we just about do. Women started using canned creamed soup in dishes in the late 1940s when they were looking for convenient shortcuts, but I recommend you make a double batch from scratch and save some for later. That way when casserole night comes along the flavors are your own, not from a can.

MAKES 4 CUPS (SERVES 4 TO 6)

4 tablespoons (½ stick) unsalted butter
4 green onions, white part only, thinly sliced
3 garlic cloves, minced
1 teaspoon chopped fresh thyme
1 pound cremini or white mushrooms, finely chopped
White pepper
2 tablespoons all-purpose flour
4 cups vegetable broth
1 cup light cream
Salt

1. In a large, heavy saucepan over medium-high heat, melt the butter. Add the green onions, garlic, and thyme and cook until the garlic is just golden, about 1 minute. (Do not overcook the garlic or it will become bitter.) Add the mushrooms and season with white pepper. Cook until the mushrooms just soften, 3 to 4 minutes.

2. Add the flour and cook, stirring constantly, until incorporated, about 1 minute. Remove from the heat and slowly stir in the broth. Return to the heat, increase the heat to high, and bring to a boil, stirring frequently. Reduce the heat and simmer gently, stirring occasionally, until slightly thickened, about 5 minutes.

3. Whisk the cream into the soup and heat gently, stirring, until hot. Do not allow the soup to boil.

4. Using an immersion blender (or in batches in a stand blender), blend until smooth. Season with salt, as needed. I often wait for this to cool and then freeze it for later use.

Sweet 'Tater SOUFFLÉ

Mashed sweet potatoes, nuts, and sugar—who doesn't love that?! This is a make-ahead and cook-it-when-you-get-home kind of dish. We like to serve this with turkey or chicken, but it really goes with everything.

SERVES 12

3 large eggs
1 cup granulated sugar
1 teaspoon pure vanilla extract
Pinch of salt
½ teaspoon black pepper
8 tablespoons (1 stick) unsalted butter, at room temperature
3 cups mashed cooked sweet potatoes (about 4 medium)
1 cup packed light brown sugar
¾ cup chopped pecans
⅓ cup cup self-rising flour (I use White Lily)

1. Preheat the oven to 350°F. Grease a 9 × 13-inch baking dish.

2. Using an electric mixer, beat together the eggs, granulated sugar, and vanilla. Add the salt, pepper, and 4 tablespoons of the butter and beat until smooth and fluffy. Fold in the mashed sweet potatoes.

3. Spread the mixture in the prepared baking dish and bake, uncovered, until firm, about 30 minutes.

4. Meanwhile, in a medium bowl, mix together the brown sugar, pecans, flour, and remaining 4 tablespoons butter with a fork until crumbly.

5. Remove the baking dish from the oven, sprinkle the topping over the sweet potatoes, and return the dish to the oven until browned and bubbling, 10 to 15 minutes longer.

Mashed 'TATERS

Yes, I said 'taters. That's what we call 'em and they are good with anything. If you have some lumps, don't fret—that's the good part.

SERVES 6

5 large russet (baking) potatoes, peeled and cut into ½-inch cubes
8 tablespoons (1 stick) unsalted butter
4 ounces cream cheese, at room temperature
½ cup heavy cream
Salt and black pepper

1. Put the potatoes in a medium pot and cover with cold water. Bring to a boil over medium-high heat and cook until fork-tender, about 30 minutes. Drain the potatoes.

2. Put the stick of butter into the hot dry pot and pour the potatoes on top. Mash the potatoes and butter together with a hand masher until the potatoes are just broken up and the butter begins to melt into the potatoes.

3. Add the cream cheese and heavy cream and beat with an electric mixer until smooth and fluffy. Add salt and pepper to taste.

Rice AND GRAVY

If there's one thing us Southerners stand by it's our gravy. We have so many different kinds, but they all start the same way—with drippings. If you're not sure what drippings are, they're those little pieces of gold stuck to the pan after you fry up your bacon, chops, cube steak, or hamburger. Or you can always start with butter. This is the simplest way I know to make gravy: equal parts of fat and flour. I'm not sure why, but my great grandma called this "'tater gravy," maybe because she poured it over 'taters.

SERVES 8

RICE

2 teaspoons salt

4 tablespoons (½ stick) unsalted butter

2 cups long-grain white rice

GRAVY

8 tablespoons (1 stick) unsalted butter

½ cup all-purpose flour

1 (32-ounce) carton chicken broth

1. Make the rice: In a large saucepan, bring 4 cups water to a boil over high heat. Add the salt and butter. When the butter has melted, add the rice, stir once, and cover. Reduce the heat to medium-low and simmer until tender and all the water has been absorbed, about 20 minutes. Fluff with a fork.

2. Meanwhile, make the gravy: In a saucepan over medium heat, melt the butter to start a roux. Whisk in the flour a little at a time until fully incorporated. Cook, whisking constantly, until the mixture reaches a peanut butter color, about 10 minutes.

3. Slowly stir in the chicken broth and then simmer until the mixture is thick and bubbling, 12 to 15 minutes.

4. Serve the gravy spooned over the rice.

Fried Green 'MATERS

Oh, nothing makes me happier than pulling a green tomato off a bush in the yard and frying it up. It's the treasure of early summer, before the tomato sandwiches and salads are a daily have-to, to cool down. The green ones that are like gold—shiny bright green with a hint of orange—are the perfect ones for frying.

SERVES 6

4 large green (unripe) tomatoes
2 large eggs
1 cup buttermilk
½ cup all-purpose flour
2 tablespoons cornmeal
Salt and black pepper
Dash of garlic powder
½ to ¾ cup peanut or vegetable oil, as needed

1. Slice the tomatoes about ¼ inch thick. Lay them all out on paper towels to drain the water out.

2. In a large bowl, beat the eggs and then whisk in the buttermilk. Submerge the tomato slices in the mixture and let sit for 15 minutes.

3. In another bowl, stir together the flour and cornmeal. Season with salt, pepper, and the garlic powder.

4. Pour enough oil into a large skillet to cover about half of each tomato slice. Heat the oil over medium-high heat.

5. Working in batches, lift the tomatoes out of the buttermilk mixture and dip them in the flour mixture. Fry each batch on both sides until golden brown, about 6 minutes total. Drain on paper towels.

Fried OKRA

I have to admit that okra is not one of my favorite things. . . . In fact, it is one of the two foods (with salmon) that I will not eat. My daughter, on the other hand, will eat fried okra faster than a T-bone steak. So in honor of my youngest child, I'd like to share her favorite way to enjoy her favorite vegetable.

SERVES 6

½ cup self-rising flour (I use White Lily)
1 cup cornmeal
1 teaspoon salt
1 teaspoon black pepper
4 cups sliced fresh okra (about 2½ pounds)
½ cup peanut or vegetable oil

1. In a large bowl, whisk together the flour, cornmeal, salt, and pepper. Add the okra and toss to make sure all the pieces are covered.

2. In a skillet over medium-high heat, heat the oil until hot. Using a slotted spoon, scoop up the okra from the bowl, shaking off any excess flour, and drop it into the hot oil. Stir occasionally and fry, in batches, until the okra is browned and crisp, about 6 minutes.

3. Remove the okra from the oil using the same slotted spoon. Drain on paper towels. Serve hot.

Fried CABBAGE

A great part of living in South Carolina is that we have the best seasons, with fruits and veggies before most of the country and long after the first frost in other places. Cabbage is something we have year-round and the heads are some of the biggest you've ever seen—up to eight or even ten pounds! This recipe is dead simple and a nice change from slaw. It's also one of my husband's favorite things in the world.

SERVES 8

4 slices bacon, chopped
1 medium head cabbage, chopped into large pieces
Salt and black pepper

1. In a large skillet over medium heat, cook the bacon until crisp, about 10 minutes. Remove the bacon to a plate.

2. Increase the heat to medium-high and toss the cabbage in the bacon drippings. Keep everything moving in the pan so the cabbage doesn't burn. The cabbage will wilt and reduce by almost half, in about 20 minutes.

3. Stir in the cooked bacon, season with salt and pepper, and serve.

Cheese Grits
FROM THE FLORIDA COAST

It wasn't until I moved to Coastal Florida at the age of eleven that I learned that cheese grits weren't just for shrimp. Every time you order any kind of seafood down there, you get cheese grits and slaw on the side. If you live in a place where you can't get grits, I say move. Grits are the food of the gods and one of the best dishes that comes from corn—aside from maybe moonshine.

SERVES 8

½ teaspoon kosher salt
2 tablespoons unsalted butter
6 small garlic cloves, minced (or to taste)
½ cup heavy cream
1 cup quick-cooking grits
2 cups shredded cheddar cheese (8 ounces)

1. In a large saucepan, bring 4 cups water to a boil over high heat. Add the salt (you must salt the grits water beforehand or you will never get enough salt in them).

2. Meanwhile, in a small skillet over medium-high heat, melt the butter. Add the garlic and cook until just tender, about 2 minutes. Remove from the heat.

3. Just as the water is about to boil in the saucepan, reduce the heat to medium. Stir in the cream and then slowly add in the grits, stirring constantly the entire time you are adding them. Keep stirring. When the grits begin to bubble, reduce the heat so that the mixture simmers, and continue cooking, stirring often, until thickened and creamy, about 5 minutes.

4. Add the garlic and butter from the skillet and stir in the cheddar until melted. Serve hot.

Peachy Praline Pie, page 164

SWEETS &
TREATS

. . . and things that go bump in your oven

As you all know, I have a hyperactive sweet tooth. If I could eat dessert and nothing else I think that would be just fine. Sweets have always been in my wheelhouse. Even though I've been baking actively since the age of four, I am still learning. In this chapter I have gathered many of what I think are the best desserts from my family. And as I've learned from years of competing and my young life at the apron strings of my nana and granny, both amazing bakers, sweets are one of the few things that will stop kids in their tracks and get them off their cell phones—at least for a short while.

PEACHY PRALINE PIE

AUNT FANNY'S BUTTERMILK PIE

Salted Chocolate Tart

MAMA'S LEMON MERINGUE PIE

BOSTON CREAM PIE (OR IS IT?)

Brown Sugar Pie

BANANA-NUT BUNDT CAKE

BUTTERMILK PECAN SKILLET CAKE

Red Velvet Cake

CHOCOLATE POUND CAKE

OREO BROWNIES

Effie's Salted Caramels

SCHOOLYARD PEANUT BUTTER BARS

TEAM REDNECK CHOCOLATE CANDY BALLS

Church Lady's Sour Cream Cookies

GERMAN CHOCOLATE COOKIES

Peachy Praline PIE

Everybody knows Georgia is the peach state, but South Carolinians grow the best peaches around, I think. Since they are one of our best summer crops, we celebrate them with a who-makes-the-best-peach-pie showdown. Not to brag, but I do. This recipe is a Blue Ribbon and Best of Show winner that I made for the Easley, South Carolina, Summer Pie Bake-off.

MAKES ONE 9-INCH PIE (SERVES 6 TO 8)

CRUST
1¼ cups all-purpose flour, plus more for rolling the dough
½ cup finely chopped pecans
½ cup butter-flavored Crisco, well chilled
¼ cup ice water

FILLING
4 cups sliced peaches
2 tablespoons fresh lemon juice
1 cup granulated sugar
Pinch of salt
3 tablespoons all-purpose flour
1½ tablespoons ground cinnamon

PRALINE
¼ cup packed light brown sugar
¼ cup granulated sugar
3 tablespoons unsalted butter, cut into pieces
1½ cups pecan pieces

1. Make the crust: Preheat the oven to 350°F.

2. In a large bowl, combine the flour, pecans, and Crisco and use a pastry blender, 2 knives, or your fingertips to mix until crumbly. Add the ice water and stir until the mixture forms a dough. Form into a ball, wrap in plastic wrap, and refrigerate for 1 hour.

3. On a lightly floured surface, roll out the dough and fit it into a 9-inch pie pan; trim and crimp the edges. Reserve the dough scraps.

4. Make the filling: In a large bowl, stir together the peaches, lemon juice, granulated sugar, salt, flour, and cinnamon until all the peach slices are well coated.

5. Make the praline: In a medium bowl, mix together the brown sugar, granulated sugar, and butter until crumbly. Add the pecan pieces and toss until coated.

6. Spread half of the praline mixture in the bottom of the pie shell and scoop the peach filling on top. Sprinkle the remaining praline mix on top. Use the scraps of crust to make cutouts of your choice to decorate the sides of the dish (peach shapes are nice!).

7. Bake until golden grown and the juices are bubbling, about 40 minutes. Let cool completely on a wire rack before serving.

Aunt Fanny's BUTTERMILK PIE

As I told y'all in the first chapter, yes, I had an aunt Fanny and the woman I knew was so cool and such a great cook. Based on what I've been told, she was pretty awesome in her heyday, too. The story goes that she survived the Great Depression by raising her kids on one income coming from sales of moonshine—and if the rumors are true it was the best 'shine in the state. (I'm glad I got to know her before she passed on, but I never did get to taste that 'shine.)

If you're not familiar with it, buttermilk pie is made with a creamy custard. Some call it sugar pie down here. Fanny's is right up there with the best of them. She always made one to keep and one to share; I do the same.

MAKES TWO 9-INCH PIES (EACH PIE SERVES 8)

6 large eggs, beaten
1 cup buttermilk
1 teaspoon pure vanilla extract
2 cups sugar
2 tablespoons cornstarch
1 teaspoon salt
1 cup (2 sticks) unsalted butter, melted
2 unbaked 9-inch deep-dish pie crusts, homemade (page 105) or store-bought

1. Preheat the oven to 350°F.

2. In a medium bowl, whisk together the eggs, buttermilk, and vanilla.

3. In a large bowl, stir together the sugar, cornstarch, and salt. Pour the melted butter on top and mix well. Pour in the egg mixture and stir until incorporated.

4. Line each of two 9-inch deep-dish pie pans with the crusts. Divide the custard mixture between the pie shells.

5. Bake until the filling is a little jiggly when you tap the pans but not runny, 50 minutes to 1 hour. Do not overbake the pies. Let cool completely on a wire rack before serving. The pies can be refrigerated overnight and brought to room temperature before serving.

Salted Chocolate TART

This is one of my most loved flavor combinations: sweet and salty. The richness of the filling just makes you moan out loud. That little bite of the salt wakes you back up from the slumber of chocolate heaven you slip into, plus you have the smooth caramel that separates the filling from the crust (and also keeps your crust from getting soggy!).

SERVES 8

CRUST

5 ounces Biscoff cookies (14 cookies)
2 tablespoons granulated sugar
¼ teaspoon flaky sea salt
6 tablespoons (¾ stick) unsalted butter, melted

FILLING

8 tablespoons (1 stick) unsalted butter
⅔ cup packed light brown sugar
1¼ cups heavy cream
1 (12-ounce) package semisweet chocolate, coarsely chopped
½ teaspoon pure vanilla extract
Flaky sea salt

1. Preheat the oven to 350°F.

2. Prepare the crust: In a food processor, pulse the cookies, granulated sugar, and salt until finely ground. Add the melted butter and pulse until combined.

3. Firmly press the crumb mixture into the bottom and up the sides of a 9-inch round or 4 × 12-inch rectangular fluted tart pan with a removable bottom. Bake until the crust is dry and set, about 12 minutes. Let cool completely on a wire rack.

4. Make the filling: In a medium saucepan over medium heat, melt the butter. Add the brown sugar and cook, whisking constantly, until the mixture begins to boil. Remove from the heat and slowly whisk in ¼ cup of the heavy cream. Set the caramel aside to cool slightly, about 15 minutes.

5. Pour the caramel into the prepared tart shell. Put in the freezer until the caramel firms up a bit but does not freeze, about 15 minutes.

6. Meanwhile, put the chocolate in a heatproof medium bowl. In a small saucepan, bring the remaining 1 cup cream to a boil. Pour the hot cream through a fine-mesh sieve over the chocolate and let sit for 2 minutes. Stir until smooth. Mix in the vanilla.

7. Pour the chocolate ganache over the top of the chilled tart and sprinkle with flaky sea salt. Let set for 2 hours and up to 6 before serving.

Mama's Lemon Meringue PIE

Oh, could Mama make a lemon meringue pie! Mama made everything well, but in all honesty, this pie may have been her shining glory. The crisp lemon flavor is to die for, so as you're making this, please think of Mama and any great cooks you've had the privilege of being fed by.

MAKES ONE 9-INCH PIE (SERVES 8)

1⅓ cups sugar
6 tablespoons cornstarch
3 large egg yolks
1 (6-ounce) can frozen lemonade, thawed
½ teaspoon salt
1 tablespoon unsalted butter, melted
1 fully baked 9-inch graham cracker pie crust, homemade
(recipe follows) or store-bought
3 large egg whites
¼ teaspoon cream of tartar

1. In a medium saucepan, mix together 1 cup of the sugar and the cornstarch. Whisk in 1½ cups cold water until combined. Bring the mixture to a boil over medium heat, stirring constantly, until the liquid is clear.

2. In a small bowl, lightly beat the egg yolks. Whisk a small amount of the hot mixture into the egg yolks (to temper them), then return the entire mixture to the saucepan. Whisk in the lemonade, salt, and melted butter.

3. Cook, whisking constantly, until thickened, about 1 minute. Do not boil. Remove from the heat, pour into

a bowl, and let cool. Once cooled, pour the filling into the prepared pie shell. Chill in the refrigerator for at least 2 hours and up to overnight.

4. Preheat the oven to 350°F.

5. Using an electric mixer, beat the egg whites with the remaining ⅓ cup sugar and the cream of tartar until stiff peaks form.

6. Spread the meringue on the pie and bake until lightly golden, about 8 minutes. Let cool completely on a wire rack and then refrigerate for at least 1 hour and up to 3 hours.

GRAHAM CRACKER PIE CRUST

1½ cups finely ground graham cracker crumbs (about 14 full-size crackers)

⅓ cup sugar

½ teaspoon ground cinnamon

8 tablespoons (1 stick) unsalted butter, melted

1. In a medium bowl, mix together the graham cracker crumbs, sugar, cinnamon, and melted butter until well blended. Press the mixture onto the bottom and all the way up the sides of an 8- or 9-inch pie pan.

2. If baking the crust before filling, preheat the oven to 350°F. Bake until deep golden brown, 8 to 10 minutes. Let cool completely in the pan on a wire rack before filling.

Boston Cream Pie (OR IS IT?)

Most of us know that Boston cream pie is really not a pie at all; it's a cake. Well, in the interest of making sure that the pie world is as respected as it should be, I have put the pie back in Boston cream pie.

MAKES ONE 10-INCH DEEP-DISH PIE (SERVES 8 TO 10)

Cooking spray
1 (16-ounce) box yellow cake mix
8 tablespoons (1 stick) unsalted butter, at room temperature
1 large egg
1½ cups heavy cream
1⅓ cups whole milk
2 (3.4-ounce) boxes French vanilla pudding
1 (12-ounce) package bittersweet chocolate, chopped
2 tablespoons light corn syrup

1. Preheat the oven to 350°F. Coat a 10-inch deep-dish pie pan with cooking spray. Coat the underside of a second 10-inch pan with cooking spray.

2. Don't read the cake box instructions. In a stand mixer fitted with the paddle attachment, beat the cake mix, butter, and egg until combined. The texture will be thick.

3. Press the cake mixture into the bottom of the prepared pan. Top with the second pan and bake until set, 9 to 11 minutes. Uncover and cool on a wire rack.

4. Using an electric mixer, whip 1 cup of the cream until stiff.

5. Using an electric mixer, beat the milk and pudding mix on the lowest speed for 2 minutes. Using a rubber spatula, fold in the whipped cream. Pour the mixture into the cooled crust, smooth the top, and chill to set, at least 2 hours and up to 4 hours.

6. Put the chocolate in a heatproof bowl. In a small saucepan, bring the remaining ½ cup cream and the corn syrup to a simmer over medium heat. Pour over the chocolate, let sit for 2 minutes, and then stir until smooth.

7. Pour the chocolate glaze over the top of the chilled pie and smooth with an offset spatula. Serve immediately.

Brown Sugar PIE

As ya'll can tell, I love the old recipes. No fancy ingredients, no searching the gourmet store aisles, no going broke to afford specialty spices. I'm all about making great food on the cheap, and this hundred-year-old recipe teaches you to make something great out of what you have at home. Every bite of this pie tastes like pure caramel.

MAKES ONE 9-INCH PIE (SERVES 8)

1 unbaked 9-inch pie crust, homemade (page 105)
or store-bought
1 cup packed light brown sugar
3 tablespoons all-purpose flour
⅛ teaspoon salt
1 cup evaporated milk
2½ tablespoons unsalted butter, cubed, at room temperature
¼ teaspoon ground cinnamon

1. Preheat the oven to 350°F.

2. In the pie shell, mix the brown sugar, flour, and salt with your fingers. Pour the evaporated milk over the flour and sugar—but *do not stir*. Drop small cubes of the butter on top of the pie. Sprinkle the cinnamon over the top.

3. Bake until the filling bubbles up in the center, about 50 minutes. The filling will not completely set, but that's how it's supposed to be. Cool completely on a wire rack. This pie is best eaten at room temperature.

Banana-Nut BUNDT CAKE

This is a soft, moist cake that is so good with coffee. It's not as dry as a nut quick bread; it's a true cake and one that I know you'll love. Nana would make this when she could buy ripe bananas on sale.

MAKES ONE 10-INCH BUNDT CAKE (SERVES 12)

3 cups sifted cake flour
1 tablespoon baking powder
1½ teaspoons baking soda
¾ teaspoon salt
¾ cup shortening (I use Crisco)
2¼ cups sugar
3 large eggs, lightly beaten
1½ cups mashed ripe bananas (about 4 bananas)
1 cup plus 2 tablespoons buttermilk
1½ teaspoons pure vanilla extract
½ cup chopped pecans

1. Preheat the oven to 375°F. Grease and flour a 10-inch Bundt pan.

2. In a large bowl, sift together the flour, baking powder, baking soda, and salt.

3. Using an electric mixer, beat the shortening until fluffy, then gradually add the sugar, continuing to beat until smooth, about 3 minutes. Add the eggs and bananas and mix well.

4. In a measuring cup or bowl, combine the buttermilk and vanilla.

5. To the banana mixture, add the flour mixture alternating with the buttermilk mixture, beginning and ending with the flour. Fold in the pecans with a rubber spatula.

6. Pour the batter into the prepared Bundt pan. Bake until golden brown on top and a toothpick inserted into the center comes out clean, 25 to 30 minutes.

7. Remove from the oven and let cool for 10 minutes in the pan. Unmold and cool completely on a wire rack. It's even better the next day; keep well wrapped at room temperature.

Buttermilk Pecan SKILLET CAKE

If Granny heard someone say "puh-CON," she would ask, "Do you see an 'o' in the word PEA-can?" This is her recipe, cooked up in a skillet, with a caramel-pecan topping that seeps down into the buttermilk cake to make it extra moist.

MAKES ONE 8-INCH SKILLET CAKE (SERVES 6 TO 8)

CAKE

1½ cups self-rising flour (I use White Lily)
½ teaspoon salt
6 tablespoons (¾ stick) unsalted butter, at room temperature
1 cup granulated sugar
1 large egg
1 large egg yolk
2 teaspoons pure vanilla extract
¾ cup buttermilk

PECAN TOPPING

¾ cup packed light brown sugar
8 tablespoons (1 stick) unsalted butter
¼ cup heavy cream
Pinch of salt
1 teaspoon pure vanilla extract
1 cup coarsely chopped pecans

1. Make the cake: Preheat the oven to 375°F. Grease and flour the bottom and sides of an 8-inch cast-iron skillet.

2. In a medium bowl, whisk together the flour and salt.

3. Using an electric mixer, beat together the butter and granulated sugar until fluffy. Add the whole egg and egg yolk, one at a time, beating for 1 minute after each addition. Mix in the vanilla.

4. With the mixer on low, add the flour mixture alternating with the buttermilk, beginning and ending with the flour, mixing well after each addition until smooth. Do not overmix. Spoon the batter, smoothing it out evenly, into the prepared skillet.

5. Bake the cake until a toothpick inserted in the center comes out clean, about 30 minutes.

6. Meanwhile, make the pecan topping: In a medium saucepan, combine the

brown sugar, butter, cream, and salt. Bring to a soft boil over medium heat and then boil, stirring constantly, for 3 minutes. Remove from the heat and stir in the vanilla and pecans. Allow to sit for about 20 minutes to thicken up a bit.

7. Pour the pecan topping over the cake while still in the skillet. Let sit until set, about 10 minutes. Once cool, this cake can be wrapped with plastic wrap and kept overnight; it's even better the next day.

Red Velvet CAKE

You're not going to find me screaming "I love red velvet cake," because, well, it's basically chocolate cake with red food coloring. But it is good to have at holidays, it takes a great picture, and everyone else seems to love it. Nana took years to perfect it and she did a great job.

MAKES ONE 8-INCH LAYER CAKE (SERVES 8 TO 10)

1 cup (2 sticks) unsalted butter, at room temperature
3 cups sugar
6 large eggs
2 tablespoons (1 ounce) red food coloring
3 cups self-rising flour (I use White Lily)
3 tablespoons unsweetened cocoa powder
1 cup buttermilk
1 teaspoon pure vanilla extract
½ teaspoon salt
Seven-Minute Icing (my choice) or Cream Cheese Frosting (recipes follow)

1. Preheat the oven to 325°F. Grease and flour three 8-inch cake pans.

2. Using an electric mixer, beat the butter with the sugar until light and creamy. Add the eggs, one at a time, beating well after each addition. Mix in the food coloring.

3. To the egg mixture, gradually add the flour and cocoa powder, alternating with the buttermilk, beginning and ending with the flour, and mixing well after each addition. Add the vanilla and salt and mix until just blended. Do not overmix or the cake will be tough.

4. Divide the batter equally between the prepared pans. Bake until a toothpick inserted in the center comes out with moist crumbs, about 25 minutes. Do not overbake. Allow to cool in the pans for 5 minutes, then unmold and cool completely on a wire rack.

5. Frost the top of each cake layer, stack them up, and then frost the sides. The cake will keep for up to 3 days.

SEVEN-MINUTE ICING

I've also heard this called crunchy icing. It turns out bright white, which is perfect for summer, and it travels well and holds up well once set. (Don't be toting it out to the picnic before it's had a chance to set up, though.) Note, however, that this icing doesn't do so well on rainy days or when it's very humid outside. My trick is to turn up the air and get the kitchen real cool before making it.

MAKES ABOUT 4 CUPS (ENOUGH TO
FROST A 2- OR 3-LAYER CAKE)

2 large egg whites
1¾ cups sugar
3 tablespoons light corn
syrup
½ teaspoon cream of tartar
¼ teaspoon salt
1½ teaspoons pure vanilla
extract

1. In a medium saucepan, bring a couple inches of water to a boil. Meanwhile, in a heatproof metal bowl, combine the egg whites, sugar, corn syrup, cream of tartar, salt, and ¼ cup water.

2. Put the bowl over the boiling water— do not let the water touch the bowl. Beat with a handheld electric mixer at high speed until the frosting forms stiff peaks, 7 to 9 minutes. Remove the bowl from the heat and stir in the vanilla.

3. Use immediately.

CREAM CHEESE FROSTING

Cream cheese frosting has got to be one of the best things invented. It's so versatile, it goes with just about every kind of cake, and the rich, creamy, smooth texture makes it super easy to spread.

MAKES 4½ CUPS (ENOUGH TO FROST A
2- OR 3-LAYER CAKE)

12 tablespoons (1½ sticks)
unsalted butter, at room
temperature
12 ounces cream cheese, at
room temperature
2 teaspoons pure vanilla
extract
6 cups powdered sugar

In a large bowl, beat together the butter, cream cheese, and vanilla until smooth. Stir in the powdered sugar, 1 cup at a time, until well combined. Use immediately.

Chocolate POUND CAKE

Julia Child once said, "A party without cake is just a meeting." I know she was right, and this cake has got to be up there with my favorites. Chocolate is the best thing on earth (right behind coffee), and I have to say this is one of the best pound cakes I've ever had. I came up with this recipe years ago when I discovered the trick to making a great pound cake: DON'T OPEN THE OVEN! If ya lookin', ya ain't cookin'.

MAKES ONE 10-INCH BUNDT CAKE (SERVES 12)

CAKE

2 cups all-purpose flour

1⅔ cups sugar

⅔ cup unsweetened cocoa powder

1 (3-ounce) box chocolate fudge instant pudding mix

2 teaspoons baking soda

1 cup sour cream

¾ cup chocolate milk

3 large eggs, lightly beaten

⅓ cup unsalted butter, melted

1 teaspoon pure vanilla extract

1 cup milk chocolate chips

1 cup semisweet chocolate chips

CHOCOLATE GLAZE

⅓ cup heavy cream

½ cup semisweet chocolate chips

1. Make the cake: Preheat the oven to 325°F. Generously grease a 10-inch Bundt pan.

2. In a large bowl, mix together the flour, sugar, cocoa powder, pudding mix, and baking soda. Mix in the sour cream, chocolate milk, eggs, melted butter, and vanilla. Stir in both kinds of chocolate chips. The batter will be very thick.

3. Spoon the batter into the prepared pan. Bake until the top springs back when touched lightly in the center and a toothpick inserted in the center comes out clean with a few moist crumbs, 55 minutes to 1 hour 5 minutes.

4. Remove from the oven and let cool for 10 minutes in the pan. Unmold and cool completely on a wire rack. This one's even better the next day; keep well wrapped at room temperature.

5. When ready to serve, make the chocolate glaze: Heat the cream in the microwave for 1 minute. Add the chips and let sit for 2 minutes. Stir until smooth and shiny. Pour the glaze over the cake and serve.

Oreo BROWNIES

Oreos are just one of the best cookies on the market—especially with all the flavors they have now. And brownies? I think I could eat one every day. (My waist wouldn't like it, but I would.) You'll love the rich chocolate brownie smoothness next to the crunch of the Oreos in this recipe. You would think the cookies would go soggy but they don't.

MAKES 12 BROWNIES

4 ounces sweet baking chocolate
8 tablespoons (1 stick) unsalted butter
2 large eggs
1½ cups self-rising flour (I use White Lily)
2 cups packed light brown sugar
¼ teaspoon salt
1 teaspoon pure vanilla extract
½ (17-ounce) package Oreo cookies, broken into big pieces

1. Preheat the oven to 350°F. Grease an 8-inch square or 9 × 13-inch baking pan.

2. In a medium saucepan, bring a couple of inches of water to a boil. In a large heatproof bowl, combine the chocolate and butter. Put the bowl over the boiling water—do not let the water touch the bowl. Heat until the chocolate and butter melt. Remove the bowl and let the mixture cool slightly.

3. Whisk the eggs, flour, brown sugar, salt, and vanilla into the chocolate mixture. Pour into the prepared pan and sprinkle the Oreos on top.

4. Bake until set and a toothpick inserted in the center comes out clean, about 30 minutes. Cool completely in the pan on a wire rack before cutting into 12 brownies.

Effie's SALTED CARAMELS

Some of you know I met Effie on the set of *The American Baking Competition*.
Even though neither one of us won, I think we came away with the biggest prize.
Baking shows come and go, but true friendships are forever. For that I am grateful
every day. And I am grateful for her absolutely perfect, soft, melt-in-your-mouth
salty caramels.

MAKES ABOUT 64 CARAMELS

Cooking spray
1 cup heavy cream
5 tablespoons unsalted butter
¼ teaspoon flaky sea salt
1 teaspoon vanilla paste or pure vanilla extract
(I use Nielsen-Massey)
1¼ cups sugar
¼ cup light corn syrup

1. Coat an 8-inch square baking pan with cooking spray and line it with parchment paper, leaving at least 1 inch overhang on two sides so you can lift out the caramels later.

2. In a medium saucepan over medium-low heat, heat the cream, butter, and salt until the butter is melted and the mixture begins to bubble up a bit. Remove from the heat and stir in the vanilla paste.

3. In a large saucepan, combine the sugar, corn syrup, and ⅓ cup water, stirring just until the sugar is dissolved. Bring to a boil over medium-low heat and cook until the syrup reaches a golden caramel color, 10 to 15 minutes.

4. Carefully add the cream mixture (the mixture will initially boil up violently) and stir together. Attach a candy thermometer to the pan and boil, stirring often, until the mixture reaches 242°F, 10 to 15 minutes.

5. Immediately remove from the heat and pour the caramel into the prepared pan. Allow to cool and set for at least 2 hours.

6. Lift the caramel out of the pan using the parchment paper and transfer to a cutting board. Coat a sharp heavy knife with cooking spray and gently cut the caramel into 1-inch squares. Wrap the caramels in small squares of wax paper. The caramels will keep in a sealed container at room temperature for up to 2 weeks.

Schoolyard PEANUT BUTTER BARS

After we lost my mother, I found this recipe stashed away on one of her shelves. For the love of peanut butter, I just knew I had to make it. These little bars melt in your mouth and taste just like the ones we all got in school when we were kids.

MAKES ABOUT 32 BARS

BARS

1 cup granulated sugar
1 cup packed light brown sugar
1 cup (2 sticks) unsalted butter, at room temperature
1 teaspoon pure vanilla extract
2 large eggs
2½ cups creamy peanut butter
2 cups old-fashioned rolled oats
2 cups all-purpose flour
1 teaspoon baking soda
1 teaspoon salt

CHOCOLATE FROSTING

8 tablespoons (1 stick) unsalted butter, at room temperature
¼ cup whole milk
1½ teaspoons pure vanilla extract
3 tablespoons unsweetened cocoa powder
2½ cups powdered sugar

1. Preheat the oven to 350°F. Grease a 13 × 18-inch jelly-roll pan or a rimmed baking sheet.

2. Make the bars: In a bowl, beat together the granulated sugar, brown sugar, and butter until smooth. Add the vanilla. Beat in the eggs, one at a time, then beat in 1 cup of the peanut butter. Mix in the oats, flour, baking soda, and salt.

3. Spread the dough out onto the prepared pan. Bake until firm, about 15 minutes.

4. Make the frosting: Using an electric mixer, combine all of the frosting ingredients and beat until smooth.

5. Remove the pan from the oven and, while still hot, spread the remaining 1½ cups peanut butter on top. Let cool until the peanut butter sets.

6. Spread the chocolate frosting on top and cut into 32 bars.

Team Redneck CHOCOLATE CANDY BALLS

This one I have to give to my buddies in "The Regal 6." I have five of the best girlfriends who have been by my side since this whole crazy thing started. This recipe came to be about two days before the three hundred-person launch party for my first cookbook. My girls and I were making some recipes from the book for the party, including Aunt Thelma's peanut butter balls. Suddenly we realized we were out of graham crackers and pecans and we were not at all close to a store. Trudy came to the rescue, pulling out some chocolate graham crackers, and I fiddled with the recipe. And guess what, a new—even simpler—recipe was born. Get Team Redneck in the kitchen and magic happens!

The addition of paraffin is perfectly safe (I've been eating it for years) and it makes the balls shiny and gets the chocolate to harden up—but you can skip it if you prefer.

MAKES ABOUT 45 BALLS

2 cups chocolate graham cracker crumbs (about 20 full crackers)
8 tablespoons (1 stick) unsalted butter, melted
1½ cups powdered sugar
2 cups creamy peanut butter
1 (16-ounce) package semisweet chocolate chips
1 ounce paraffin wax, grated (optional)

1. In a large bowl, mix together the graham cracker crumbs, melted butter, powdered sugar, and peanut butter. Using your hands, roll the mixture into 1-inch balls, arrange on a baking sheet lined with wax paper, and refrigerate until firm, about 20 minutes.

2. Melt the chocolate in the microwave or on the stovetop. Add the paraffin (if using) and stir well to make sure it's melted. Spear a ball with a toothpick, dip the ball in the chocolate to coat, and then return the ball to the baking sheet, removing the toothpick. Repeat with the remaining balls. Once all the balls are coated, chill them in the refrigerator until hardened, about 30 minutes.

3. Store in an airtight container in the refrigerator for up to 2 weeks; serve chilled.

Church Lady's
SOUR CREAM COOKIES

I bet this is one of those recipes that was so good people tried to hide it—but then it got out and was passed around because everybody loves these really rich sugar cookies. This recipe makes enough to keep all the kids in children's church quiet 'til the preaching stops.

MAKES ABOUT 5 DOZEN COOKIES

COOKIES

1 cup (2 sticks) unsalted butter, at room temperature
2 cups granulated sugar
3 large eggs, lightly beaten
1 cup sour cream
1 teaspoon pure vanilla extract
5 cups all-purpose flour
1 tablespoon baking powder
½ teaspoon baking soda

FROSTING

4 tablespoons (½ stick) unsalted butter, at room temperature
1 cup powdered sugar
Pinch of salt
1 teaspoon pure vanilla extract
1½ teaspoons whole milk

1. Make the cookies: Preheat the oven to 350°F. Grease 2 baking sheets.

2. Using an electric mixer, beat the butter and granulated sugar until fluffy. Add the eggs, mix well, then beat in the sour cream and vanilla.

3. Sift together the flour, baking powder, and baking soda into a bowl. Add the flour mixture to the egg mixture, mixing until just combined.

4. Working in batches, drop the batter by the tablespoon onto the prepared baking sheets, leaving space between the cookies. Bake until golden around the edges and just set in the centers, 10 to 12 minutes. Transfer the cookies to a wire rack to cool completely.

5. Make the frosting: In a medium bowl, beat together the butter, powdered sugar, salt, vanilla, and milk until smooth. Frost the cookies with the mixture and let set, at least 10 minutes.

German Chocolate COOKIES

If you like German chocolate cake—full of rich chocolate flavor, nuts, and coconut—you're going to have to try these. I came across this recipe in an old cookbook from the Jockey Lot (which is a huge local flea market). The book is filled with loosely written (by today's standards) recipes, and has a ragged, heavily used appearance, which is not surprising as it was printed back in 1925. That's almost one hundred years old, so you know this has to be good! I did a little fiddling with the recipe so it comes out right every time.

MAKES 2 DOZEN COOKIES

8 tablespoons (1 stick) unsalted butter, at room temperature
¼ cup granulated sugar
½ cup packed light brown sugar
½ teaspoon pure vanilla extract
1 large egg
1 cup all-purpose flour
¼ cup unsweetened cocoa powder
½ teaspoon baking soda
½ teaspoon salt
1 cup bittersweet or semisweet chocolate chips
½ cup chopped toasted pecans
¾ cup unsweetened shredded coconut (toasted, if you'd like)

1. Preheat the oven to 350°F. Grease 2 baking sheets.

2. Using an electric mixer, beat the butter, granulated sugar, and brown sugar until light and fluffy. Add the vanilla and egg and mix until well combined.

3. In a medium bowl, whisk together the flour, cocoa powder, baking soda, and salt. Add to the butter mixture and mix until just combined. Using a rubber spatula, fold in the chocolate chips, pecans, and coconut.

4. Drop the batter by the tablespoon onto the prepared sheets, leaving a 2-inch space between the cookies. Bake until puffed up and browned on top, about 10 minutes. Transfer the cookies to a wire rack to cool completely.

Upside-Down Apple Bacon
Pie, page 206

HOLIDAY
BAKED GOODS

To bring a family together

During the holidays I spend extra time in the kitchen, baking for my family. It's the one time of year around here that it's cool enough to crank the oven up for hours on end! In this chapter you'll find recipes for some of my favorite festive baked goods. Or, if you're feeling frisky, you can make 'em whenever just to show people you care enough about them to log some time in your kitchen. Your family will know what's going on when they walk in the house and smell everything good baking in the oven.

Easy Yeast Rolls, page 194

Easy Yeast ROLLS

Any recipe with yeast in it can be overwhelming or scary to some folks. But I promise this is one of the easiest ways to make yeast rolls you'll ever come across. These are almost what people would call steakhouse rolls—you know those rolls they bring you to eat with honey butter so that you're too full to eat your steak and it goes home in a to-go box? These are that good.

MAKES 24 ROLLS

¾ cup whole milk
½ cup sugar
1 teaspoon salt
2 large eggs, lightly beaten
5 teaspoons active dry yeast (I buy it in bulk)
5 cups all-purpose flour, plus more as needed
8 tablespoons (1 stick) unsalted butter, melted

1. In a saucepan, combine ¾ cup water, the milk, sugar, and salt and heat over low heat until lukewarm (about 120°F). Remove from the heat and mix in the eggs and yeast.

2. Put the flour in a large bowl. Make a well in the center and pour in the warm liquid mixture. Do not stir. Cover with a lid or plastic wrap and let sit until doubled in size, 20 to 30 minutes.

3. Pour in the melted butter and mix well. If the dough is sticky, add more flour until the dough is soft but no longer sticky. Knead several times by hand on a lightly floured surface. Return to the bowl and cover again with the lid. Let the dough sit until puffed back up, another 20 to 30 minutes.

4. Preheat the oven to 400°F. Grease 2 baking sheets.

5. Divide the dough into 12 equal pieces and then divide each piece in half to make 24. Shape each one into a ball and arrange 1½ inches apart on the prepared baking sheets. Cover with a clean damp kitchen towel or a greased piece of plastic wrap and let rise until doubled in size, 20 to 30 minutes.

6. Uncover and bake until golden brown, about 15 minutes. Cool at least slightly on a wire rack before serving warm or at room temperature.

Cranberry BREAD

Those tart, hard little berries that bob in flooded fields can become sweet, textured little gems of awesome if you treat 'em right. I like them year-round (I freeze fresh ones every winter just to keep on hand), but if you don't, you can change the cranberries up with blueberries or chopped strawberries instead.

MAKES ONE 9 × 5-INCH LOAF (SERVES 10)

2 cups all-purpose flour
1 cup sugar
1½ teaspoons baking powder
½ teaspoon baking soda
½ teaspoon salt
1 large egg, well beaten
2 tablespoons unsalted butter, melted
2 tablespoons hot water
¼ cup grated orange zest
½ cup fresh orange juice (about 3 medium oranges)
1 cup fresh cranberries, dusted in flour

1. Preheat the oven to 325°F. Grease a 9 × 5-inch loaf pan.

2. In a large bowl, sift together the flour, sugar, baking powder, baking soda, and salt. Add the egg, melted butter, hot water, orange zest, and orange juice and stir until combined. Using a rubber spatula, fold in the cranberries. The batter will be very thick.

3. Scoop the batter into the prepared pan and smooth out the top. Bake until golden brown and a toothpick inserted into the center comes out clean, about 1 hour. Cool for 10 minutes in the pan, then unmold and cool completely on a wire rack.

Strawberry Custard TRIFLE

Yes, this sounds fancy because it's a trifle, but trust me that it's beyond easy and pure redneck. I layer the cake, strawberries, pudding, and topping in mason jars, set these out at parties, and watch them disappear. Bask in the compliments and don't tell anyone your secret—packaged ingredients artfully put together.

SERVES 8 TO 10

1 (15-ounce) box yellow or white cake mix
3 large eggs
⅓ cup vegetable oil
1 (5-ounce) box vanilla instant pudding mix
2 cups whole milk
1 (16-ounce) package frozen strawberries with syrup, thawed (or use fresh strawberries, sliced and sweetened)
1 (12-ounce) container frozen whipped topping, thawed

1. Make the cake batter as directed using the eggs and oil and bake in a 9 × 13-inch pan. Let cool completely in the pan. Cut the cake into 1-inch squares.

2. Prepare the vanilla pudding as directed using the milk.

3. Arrange a layer of cake in 8 to 10 one-pint canning jars (or in a 2-quart glass trifle bowl). Pour half of the strawberries with their syrup over the cake. Divide 1 cup of the pudding on top. Repeat with the remaining cake pieces, strawberries, and pudding. Spread the whipped topping over the top. Chill thoroughly, at least 1 hour and up to overnight.

Pumpkin Roll CAKE

Now I have to say pumpkin is one of my all-time favorite flavors and I really could eat pumpkin stuff year-round. I just don't tire of it. Here I roll it up (with cream cheese, of course) in a jelly-roll cake, which is one of those things that impresses people. You can always find these kinds of "roulades" in bakeries, but they're worth making at home yourself.

SERVES 10

CAKE

Cooking spray

3 large eggs, separated

1 cup granulated sugar

⅔ cup canned unsweetened pumpkin puree (not pumpkin pie mix)

¾ cup all-purpose flour

1 teaspoon baking soda

½ teaspoon ground cinnamon

⅛ teaspoon salt

Powdered sugar, as needed

FILLING

8 ounces cream cheese, at room temperature

2 tablespoons unsalted butter, at room temperature

1 cup powdered sugar

¾ teaspoon pure vanilla extract

1. Make the cake: Preheat the oven to 375°F. Coat an 11 × 15-inch jelly-roll pan or rimmed baking sheet with cooking spray and then line with parchment paper.

2. Using an electric mixer, beat the egg yolks on high speed until thick and lemon colored. Gradually add ½ cup of the granulated sugar and the pumpkin, beating on high until the sugar is almost dissolved.

3. Clean your beaters and use them to whip the egg whites until soft peaks form. Gradually add the remaining ½ cup granulated sugar, beating until stiff peaks form. Gently fold the egg whites into the pumpkin mixture.

4. In a medium bowl, whisk together the flour, baking soda, cinnamon, and salt. Gently fold the flour mixture into the pumpkin mixture.

5. Spread the pumpkin batter into the prepared pan, smoothing the top. Bake until the cake springs back when lightly touched, 12 to 15 minutes.

6. Remove from the oven and let cool for just 5 minutes. Dust a clean kitchen towel with powdered sugar. Turn the cake out onto the towel and gently peel off the parchment paper. With one of the long sides facing you, roll the cake up in the towel. Cool completely on a wire rack, still rolled up.

7. Make the filling: In a small bowl, beat the cream cheese, butter, powdered sugar, and vanilla until smooth.

8. Unroll the cake and spread the filling evenly over it to within ½ inch of the edges. Trim the ends so the filling shows and the ends are even. Roll up again the same way, wrap in plastic wrap, and chill until firm, at least 2 hours and up to overnight.

9. Unwrap, cut into 10 slices, and serve.

Sweet Potato SPICE CAKE

Don't be afraid of sweet potatoes in a cake! Think about it: They go so well with nutmeg, cinnamon, and cloves. Plus, they give their pretty color to this cake, which has the light, airy texture of a chiffon cake.

MAKES ONE 8-INCH LAYER CAKE (SERVES 8)

2½ cups all-purpose flour
¼ teaspoon salt
3 tablespoons baking powder
1 teaspoon ground nutmeg
¼ teaspoon ground cloves
1 teaspoon ground cinnamon
1½ cups vegetable oil
2 cups sugar
1 teaspoon pure vanilla extract
4 large eggs, separated
¼ cup hot water
1½ cups grated peeled sweet potatoes
½ cup chopped pecans
Cream Cheese Frosting (page 179)

1. Preheat the oven to 350°F. Grease and flour three 8-inch cake pans.

2. In a large bowl, sift together the flour, salt, baking powder, nutmeg, cloves, and cinnamon.

3. Using an electric mixer, beat together the oil, sugar, and vanilla until smooth. Add the egg yolks, one at a time, and beat well. Whisk in the hot water followed by the flour mixture. Using a rubber spatula, fold in the sweet potatoes and pecans

4. Clean the mixer beaters and use them to whip the egg whites until stiff peaks form. Use a rubber spatula to fold the whites into the batter. Divide the batter evenly among the prepared cake pans.

5. Bake until golden brown and a toothpick inserted in the center comes out clean, 25 to 30 minutes. Cool in the pans on a wire rack for 12 minutes, then remove from the pans and let cool completely on the rack.

6. Frost the top of each cake layer, stack them up, and then frost the sides. The cake will keep, under a cake dome, for up to 3 days at room temperature.

Date Nut CAKE

Two blocks away from the house I grew up in there was a little bakery owned by a man so short he could barely see over the counter. Every day we would go there after school and he would meet us with a lemon bar for me and a piece of date cake for Mama. After years of this, when Mama told him we were moving, he gave her the date nut cake recipe, which inspired this simple cake. The only other thing I will say about this cake is if you don't love dates you will after you eat this.

SERVES 9

1 cup chopped pitted dates
1 cup boiling water
1 teaspoon baking soda
1 tablespoon unsalted butter
1 cup sugar
½ teaspoon salt
1 large egg, lightly beaten
1 teaspoon pure vanilla extract
½ cup chopped walnuts
1½ cups all-purpose flour
Sugar Glaze Icing (optional; recipe follows)

1. Preheat the oven to 350°F. Butter and flour an 8-inch square baking pan.

2. In a large bowl, stir together dates, boiling water, baking soda, and butter. Set aside to cool.

3. Mix in the sugar, salt, egg, vanilla, walnuts, and flour. The batter will be slightly thick. Spoon the batter into the prepared pan.

4. Bake until a toothpick inserted in the center comes out clean, 40 to 50 minutes. Cool for 10 minutes in the pan, then unmold and cool completely on a wire rack.

5. If desired, pour the sugar glaze over the cake. Cut into 9 slices.

SUGAR GLAZE ICING

MAKES ABOUT 1 CUP

1 cup powdered sugar
2 tablespoons heavy cream
½ teaspoon pure vanilla
extract

In a bowl, whisk together the sugar, cream, and vanilla until smooth.

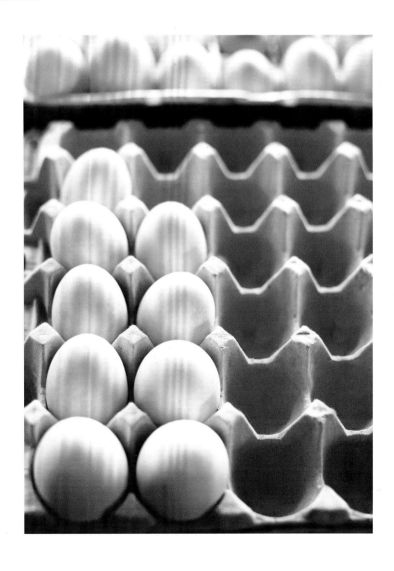

Apple Almond TART

This recipe is my version of a tart I once had at a fancy grocery store. You know the ones where everything looks like you're standing in a fancy bakery in Paris? Until I get to Paris, which is on my bucket list, I go into those to be inspired. So stick that pinkie up and make a tart!

MAKES ONE 9- OR 10-INCH TART (SERVES 8 TO 10)

TART SHELL

1½ cups all-purpose flour, plus more for rolling the dough

6 tablespoons sugar

¼ teaspoon salt

8 tablespoons (1 stick) cold unsalted butter, cut into cubes

1 large egg, lightly beaten

ALMOND FILLING

⅔ cup blanched slivered almonds

½ cup sugar

6 tablespoons (¾ stick) unsalted butter, at room temperature

1 large egg, lightly beaten

1 egg yolk

1 teaspoon vanilla paste

2 tablespoons all-purpose flour

3 to 4 medium baking apples, as needed

⅓ cup apricot preserves

4 teaspoons bourbon

Chopped almonds, for garnish (optional)

1. Make the tart shell: In a food processor, combine the flour, sugar, and salt and process for 2 to 3 seconds. Scatter the butter pieces over the mixture. Pulse on and off until the mixture resembles coarse meal.

2. Add the egg and pulse on and off again. The dough should form sticky crumbs that can be easily pressed together. If the dough is dry, add ½ teaspoon cold water and quickly process again.

3. Transfer the dough to a floured work surface. Shape into a flat disc, wrap in plastic wrap, and refrigerate for at least 1 hour and up to 2 days.

4. Remove the dough from the refrigerator and let soften for 5 minutes.

5. Roll the dough on a lightly floured surface into a ¼-inch-thick round. Roll the dough loosely around the rolling pin and then unroll it over a 9- or 10-inch round metal tart pan with a removable bottom. Press into the sides of the pan and trim the edges. Cover and refrigerate for at least 1 hour or up to 3 hours.

6. Preheat the oven to 350°F.

7. Make the almond filling: In a food processor, grind the slivered almonds and 2 tablespoons of the sugar to a fine powder.

8. Using an electric mixer, beat the butter until soft. Add the remaining 6 tablespoons sugar and beat until the mixture is fluffy. Gradually beat in the beaten egg and egg yolk. Stir in the almond mixture, the vanilla paste, and flour. Spread the almond filling evenly over the bottom of the prepared pastry shell.

9. Peel, core, and halve the apples. Arrange each half cut-side down and cut into thin slices, keeping each half together. Using a metal spatula, transfer the sliced apple half to the top of the almond filling and fan out the slices in a circle so they radiate outward from the center like spokes on a wheel. Press slightly to flatten out the slices.

10. Bake until the almond filling is set and golden brown, about 30 minutes. Cool completely on a wire rack.

11. In a small saucepan over low heat, heat the preserves and bourbon, stirring often, until melted. Strain the mixture and then brush the glaze over the top of the tart. Sprinkle a few chopped almonds over the top, if desired.

Upside-Down APPLE BACON PIE

This is a variation on the pecan upside-down pie in my first cookbook. Instead of painstakingly placing the pecans as for that pie, you get to weave bacon together to crown the pie. Yes, I said bacon. It's like serving applesauce with pork chops, only sweeter and better. And, as with the pecan pie, store-bought dough is the way to go here; it stands up better and gives the pie more structure.

MAKES ONE 9-INCH DEEP-DISH PIE (SERVES 8 TO 10)

8 tablespoons (1 stick) unsalted butter, at room temperature
1½ cups packed light brown sugar
1 (16-ounce) package thick-cut bacon
2 unbaked 9-inch refrigerated pie crusts
(I use store-bought for this recipe)
3 tablespoons all-purpose flour
½ cup granulated sugar
1⅛ teaspoons ground cinnamon
½ teaspoon ground nutmeg
1 tablespoon apple pie spice
1 teaspoon pure vanilla extract
2 tablespoons fresh lemon juice
6 cups peeled, cored, sliced baking apples, such as
Granny Smith

1. Preheat the oven to 450°F.

2. Grease the bottom and sides of a 9-inch deep-dish pie pan with the entire stick of butter. Sprinkle and dust 1 cup of the brown sugar into the pan until the whole inside of the pan is covered, bottom and sides.

3. Weave the raw bacon tightly together to make a 12-inch lattice. (Remember the pot holders everyone used to make? Well, this is kind of like that.) Press the bacon into the pan on top of the brown sugar. Put one pie crust on top of the bacon and press on it until it molds to the bottom of the pan. Do not trim the edges just yet.

4. In a large bowl, mix together the flour, granulated sugar, remaining ½ cup brown sugar, the cinnamon, nutmeg, apple pie spice, vanilla, and lemon juice. Add the sliced apples and toss to coat. Scoop the filling into the pie crust, spreading it out as evenly as you can. Cover with the second pie crust. Press the edges of the two crusts

together and crimp to seal. Don't worry about looks; this is the bottom of your pie. Poke a dozen holes at random with a fork for steam.

5. Bake for 10 minutes. Reduce the oven temperature to 350°F and bake until the sides are bubbling, 45 minutes longer.

6. Remove from the oven and let sit just until the bubbling stops, about 5 minutes. Important: You must flip this over onto a serving plate while it's still hot. Put a plate over the pie, grab the pie and plate with two pot holders, and invert. Remove the pie pan. Let cool on the plate before serving.

Peppermint CAKE

Last June, I was asked to do a magazine shoot for Christmas. (I learned *all* those beautiful Christmas magazines I read are shot during the summer!) Y'all know how hard it is to find candy canes in June? I borrowed Christmas trees from my friend Deena who found them that week at a thrift shop. Then I turned down my AC with the thought of building a fire in the fireplace. We made my little trailer kitchen into a full studio and boy was it fun. This is the cake I made. It's so pretty and it tastes so good—and if you keep candy canes around, you can pull this off any time, too!

MAKES ONE 9-INCH LAYER CAKE (SERVES 12)

CAKE
1 cup (2 sticks) unsalted butter, at room temperature
2 cups sugar
4 large eggs
3 cups sifted self-rising flour (I use White Lily)
1 cup whole milk
1 teaspoon pure vanilla extract
½ teaspoon peppermint extract
4 drops red food coloring

ICING
2 large egg whites
1½ cups sugar
1½ tablespoons light corn syrup
¼ teaspoon cream of tartar
Pinch of salt
1½ teaspoons pure vanilla extract

Peppermint candies, for garnish (optional)

1. Make the cake: Preheat the oven to 350°F. Grease and flour two 9-inch cake pans.

2. Using an electric mixer, beat the butter until creamy. Add the sugar and continue to beat until fluffy. Add the eggs, one at a time. Add the flour alternating with the milk, beginning and ending with the flour. Add the vanilla and beat until just combined.

3. Pour half of the batter into a clean bowl and stir in the peppermint extract and red food coloring.

4. Pour a small round of white batter into each pan and then pour some of the red batter on top in the center. Alternate these layers of colors 4 times until the pans look like bull's-eyes.

5. Bake until a toothpick inserted in the center comes out clean, 30 to 35 minutes. Cool in the pans for 5 to 10 minutes before unmolding onto a wire rack to cool completely.

6. Make the icing: Bring a couple inches of water to a boil in a medium saucepan. In a heatproof bowl, combine the egg whites, sugar, corn syrup, cream of tartar, salt, and $1/3$ cup water. Put the bowl over the boiling water—do not let the water touch the bowl. Beat with a handheld electric mixer at high speed until the frosting forms stiff peaks, 7 to 9 minutes.

7. Stir in the vanilla. Frost the top of each cake layer, stack them up, and then frost the sides. Sprinkle the candies on top of the cake, if desired. The cake will keep, under a cake dome, for up to 2 days at room temperature.

Holiday WHOOPIES

I love whoopie pies. They're one of those desserts that just tickles me. I enjoy them in any flavor, but I make red velvet over the holidays because they look so good on a plate. This recipe is slightly different from the one for the cake, with brown sugar for a more intense flavor and a denser texture as well to help the whoopies keep their shape.

MAKES 15 WHOOPIE PIES

WHOOPIE PIES

2 cups self-rising flour (I use White Lily)
2 tablespoons unsweetened cocoa powder
Pinch of salt
8 tablespoons (1 stick) unsalted butter, at room temperature
1 cup packed light brown sugar
1 large egg
1 teaspoon pure vanilla extract
½ cup buttermilk
2 tablespoons (1 ounce) red food coloring

FILLING

4 tablespoons (½ stick) unsalted butter, at room temperature
1 teaspoon pure vanilla extract
4 ounces cream cheese, at room temperature
1 (7-ounce) jar marshmallow creme (I like Fluff)
1 cup heavy cream

12 candy canes

1. Make the whoopie pies: Preheat the oven to 375°F. Line 2 baking sheets with parchment paper.

2. In a medium bowl, combine the flour, cocoa powder, and salt.

(recipe continues)

3. Using an electric mixer, beat the butter on medium-high for 30 seconds. Beat in the brown sugar until light and fluffy. Beat in the egg and vanilla. Add the flour mixture alternating with the buttermilk, beginning and ending with the flour mixture, mixing well after each addition. Mix in the food coloring. Do not overmix.

4. Use a cookie scoop to portion the batter in 2-inch rounds and arrange 1 inch apart on the prepared baking sheets. You should have 30 rounds.

5. Bake until the tops are set and spring back when touched gently, 9 to 11 minutes. Allow to cool completely on the baking sheets on a rack. Remove the cooled cookies from the baking sheets.

6. Make the filling: Using an electric mixer, beat the butter until smooth. Add the vanilla and cream cheese and beat until smooth. Using a rubber spatula, fold in the marshmallow creme. Add the heavy cream and beat on high for about 1 minute until doubled in size. Scoop the filling into a piping bag (or a zip-top bag with one corner cut off). Pipe the filling onto the flat side of half of the whoopies and top each with a second whoopie, flat side down.

7. Put the candy canes in a plastic bag and crush with a rolling pin into bits. Roll the sides of the whoopies into the crushed candy. The whoopie pies will keep covered in the refrigerator for up to 3 days.

Fruitcake THAT AIN'T HEAVY

I have here a fruitcake that cannot be used as a doorstop. It's not that heavy, bulky cake that almost everyone hates. This one is light and lovable—trust me!

MAKES ONE 8-INCH LOAF (SERVES 8)

¼ cup diced candied lemon peel
½ cup diced candied pineapple
¾ cup whole candied cherries
1 cup chopped pecans or walnuts
1½ cups all-purpose flour
½ teaspoon baking powder
1 teaspoon salt
½ cup vegetable oil
¾ cup sugar
2 large eggs
½ cup pineapple or apple juice
1 cup brandy

1. Preheat the oven to 350°F. Grease an 8 × 5-inch loaf pan. Line the bottom and two long sides with parchment paper.

2. In a large bowl, mix together the lemon peel, candied pineapple, cherries, nuts, and ½ cup of the flour.

3. In a medium bowl, sift together the remaining 1 cup flour, the baking powder, and salt.

4. In another medium bowl, whisk together the oil, sugar, and eggs. Beat vigorously for 2 minutes. Gradually stir the oil mixture into the flour mixture, alternating with the pineapple juice. Pour the batter over the floured fruit and mix thoroughly.

5. Pour the battered fruit into the prepared pan. Bake until browned on top and a toothpick inserted in the center comes out clean, about 45 minutes.

6. Let the cake cool in the pan for 15 minutes. Pour the brandy over the cake and let sit until completely cool.

7. Unmold the cake, remove the parchment paper, and wrap the cake tightly in foil. It will keep for up to 3 days at room temperature; if you'd like to keep it longer, freeze it for up to 3 months.

Peach Bread,
page 232

BREADS & ROLLS

'Cause everyone loves a few carbs

Breads are one of those things that took me a while to learn how to do right. Some things I still have a little tweaking to do on, but all in all this chapter should take the fear out of bread for y'all. I have found over the years that bread baking can even be therapeutic, and it definitely satisfies my drive to keep learning in the kitchen.

BUTTERMILK ROLLS

LEMONADE ROLLS

Sweet Potato Biscuits

PIMENTO BISCUITS

EFFIE'S CREAMED BISCUITS

1940s Batter Bread

PEANUT BUTTER MUFFINS

OATMEAL BREAD

Banana Nut Bread

BLACKBERRY PECAN BREAD

PEACH BREAD

Orange Nut Loaf

Buttermilk ROLLS

My great-granny was the buttermilk queen. I mean, this woman used buttermilk in everything, including rolls, cakes, and cookies. If something called for milk, she used buttermilk. She would even drink it straight. When I would see her fixing to make these, I knew I was in for a treat—and a little work. Great-Granny would sucker me into making homemade butter with a real butter churn, no mixers. We'd sit out on the porch churning butter (to slather on top of the hot rolls) and buttermilk (to bake with), watching the cars go by. Yep, those were the days.

MAKES 22 ROLLS

1 (0.25-ounce) envelope active dry yeast
¼ cup warm water (110° to 115°F)
2½ cups all-purpose flour, plus more for kneading the dough
¼ teaspoon baking soda
1 teaspoon salt
1 tablespoon sugar
¾ cup lukewarm buttermilk
3 tablespoons shortening (I use Crisco), at room temperature

1. In a large bowl, dissolve the yeast in the water.

2. In a separate bowl, mix together 1¼ cups of the flour with the baking soda, and salt. Add the flour mixture, sugar, buttermilk, and shortening to the yeast and mix well with a wooden spoon. Add the remaining 1¼ cups flour and mix well until it comes together.

3. Turn the dough out onto a floured surface and knead about 4 times until smooth. Shape into 1½-inch rolls. Put them close to one another on a greased baking sheet in 2 rows of 11 rolls so that they almost touch (and will touch once they rise). Let them rise until doubled in volume, about 1 hour 15 minutes.

4. Preheat the oven to 400°F.

5. Bake the rolls until golden brown, 15 to 20 minutes. Let cool slightly before serving warm or at room temperature.

Lemonade ROLLS

There was a little lady who lived down the street from us when I was a kid in Greenville who would make these about twice a month. When she saw us kids out riding our bikes she would holler at us to come get a lemonade roll. Before the lady passed she gave her recipe to Mama. I can't tell you where the recipe came from originally, but I can tell you that these are one of the best things I have ever had.

MAKES 10 SPIRAL ROLLS

2 (0.25-ounce) envelopes active dry yeast
2½ cups warm water (110° to 115°F)
5 cups all-purpose flour, plus more for rolling the dough
1 (18.25-ounce) box lemon cake mix
2 teaspoons kosher salt
6 tablespoons (¾ stick) unsalted butter, at room temperature
⅓ cup Country Time Lemonade drink mix powder
2 cups powdered sugar
3 to 4 fresh tablespoons lemon juice, as needed

1. In a medium bowl, stir together the yeast and water.

2. In a stand mixer fitted with the dough hook attachment, mix together the flour, cake mix, and salt. Add the yeast mixture and continue mixing until the ingredients are combined and start to form a ball. Remove the bowl from the mixer. Cover with a clean towel and set in a warm spot to rise for 1 hour.

3. Grease two 9 × 13-inch baking pans.

4. Roll out the dough on a floured surface into a rectangle about 10 × 24 inches. Spread the butter over the dough and sprinkle the lemonade mix over it. With a short side facing you, roll the dough up into a 10-inch-long log, leaving it seam-side down. With a serrated knife, gently cut the log crosswise into ten 1-inch slices. Arrange 5 slices in each prepared pan. Cover with a clean towel and again set in a warm spot to rise until doubled in volume, about 1 hour.

5. Preheat the oven to 350°F.

6. Bake until the rolls are golden brown, 20 to 25 minutes.

7. Meanwhile, in a medium bowl, stir together the powdered sugar and lemon juice until smooth and pourable.

8. Pour the glaze over the warm rolls. Serve warm or at room temperature.

FRESH "CHURNED" BUTTER, MY WAY

We don't churn butter the way I did with my great-granny anymore. Now I've learned to do it the easy way: in a stand mixer. Just add the desired amount of heavy cream with a sprinkling of salt and whip the cream until it separates. Keep mixing until butter forms and the liquid will fall to the bottom of the bowl. Scoop out the butter, wrap it tightly in plastic, and chill. For every cup of heavy cream, you'll get about 4 tablespoons (½ stick) butter.

Sweet Potato BISCUITS

Yes, we put sweet 'taters in a biscuit. We'll put just about anything in a biscuit as long as it tastes good, but then again I have no clue what'd taste bad in a biscuit. The sweet potatoes give the biscuits a flavor that's sweet and tart—and is hard to put your finger on if you don't know what's in the mix. Serve these warm with fresh butter and a sprinkle of cinnamon sugar on a cold morning.

MAKES 12 BISCUITS

1 cup all-purpose flour, plus more for working with the dough
3 teaspoons baking powder
2 teaspoons light brown sugar
1 teaspoon salt
½ teaspoon ground nutmeg
3 tablespoons shortening (I use Crisco)
¾ cup mashed cooked sweet potatoes
¼ cup whole milk, or as needed

1. Preheat the oven to 400°F. Grease a baking sheet.

2. In a medium bowl, stir together the flour, baking powder, brown sugar, salt, and nutmeg. Cut the shortening into the flour mixture using a pastry blender, 2 knives, or your fingertips until the shortening bits are the size of peas. Mix in the sweet potatoes and add enough of the milk to make a soft dough.

3. Turn the dough out onto a floured surface and pat it out until it's ¾ inch thick. Cut it into 2-inch rounds using a biscuit cutter or cut into 2-inch squares. Gather the scraps and re-pat the dough to cut out more biscuits. Put the biscuits 1 inch apart onto the prepared baking sheet.

4. Bake until golden brown, 12 to 15 minutes. Let cool at least slightly before serving warm or at room temperature.

Pimento BISCUITS

I don't know who in the world thought putting pimentos with cheese was a good idea, but they were wrong—it's a *great* idea. Putting it in a biscuit? Wait . . . can you hear that? It's angels singing. You put a little piece of country ham on these and the whole church choir just jumps to their feet. Drizzle the biscuits with red-eye gravy and, have mercy, there are no words! Plus, they are perfect cold, packed in the lunch bag as you're heading out to go fishing.

MAKES ABOUT 15 BISCUITS

```
2 cups all-purpose flour, plus more for rolling the dough
1 tablespoon baking powder
¼ teaspoon baking soda
½ teaspoon salt
½ cup shortening (I use Crisco) or lard
1 cup of your favorite pimento cheese
¾ to 1 cup buttermilk, as needed
4 tablespoons (½ stick) unsalted butter, melted
```

1. Preheat the oven to 450°F.

2. In a large bowl, whisk together the flour, baking powder, baking soda, and salt. Cut the shortening into the flour mixture with a pastry blender, 2 knives, or your fingertips until the shortening bits are the size of peas. Add the pimento cheese. Stirring with a fork, add enough buttermilk until the mixture leaves the sides of the bowl and forms a soft, moist dough.

3. On a floured surface, roll the dough around until it's no longer sticky. Roll the dough out until it is ½ inch thick. Cut out 2-inch rounds with a biscuit cutter and arrange on an ungreased baking sheet leaving space between the biscuits.

4. Bake until golden brown on top, about 10 minutes. Brush with the melted butter and serve hot.

Effie's Creamed BISCUITS

I really do thank God every day that Effie and I became friends. People ask me, "When we saw y'all arm and arm on TV, was that just for TV?" Nope. We talk all the time, share recipes, laugh, cry, and even travel with our families to split the distance between us just to be together. So when she called and said I made these biscuits and they're awesome, I listened. I think she may have discovered the best and easiest biscuit recipe the world has ever seen.

MAKES 12 BISCUITS

1¼ cups plus 2 tablespoons heavy cream
2¼ cups self-rising flour, plus more for dusting
(I use White Lily)

1. Preheat the oven to 450°F. Line a baking sheet with parchment paper.

2. Put 1¼ cups of the heavy cream in the freezer for 15 minutes so it gets really cold.

3. Put the flour in a medium bowl and whisk to make sure there are no lumps. Using a rubber spatula, stir in the 1¼ cups cold heavy cream until just combined. The dough will be sticky.

4. Dust a work surface with flour and rub your hands with some flour as well. Gather the dough to the center of the bowl and then turn the dough onto the surface. Gently bring it together into a ball and then flatten it into a rough disc. Fold one half over the other and then gently pat the dough into a 7-inch square.

5. Using a sharp knife, cut the dough into 12 squares (3 rows of 4 biscuits). Put the biscuit squares on the prepared baking sheet and brush with the remaining 2 tablespoons cream.

6. Bake until light golden brown, 11 to 13 minutes. Serve immediately.

1940s *Batter Bread*

This is an oldie but goodie. You know, the kind that makes you think of June Cleaver vacuuming in heels? Or Aunt Bee getting groceries delivered by a boy on a bike with a bow tie? Well, this is that kind of recipe, a tried-and-true, good old-fashioned loaf bread perfect for sandwiches.

MAKES ONE 9-INCH LOAF

½ cup whole milk, scalded
1½ tablespoons sugar
½ tablespoon salt
1 tablespoon butter, at room temperature
½ cup warm water (105° to 115°F)
1 (0.25-ounce) envelope active dry yeast
2¼ cups all-purpose flour

1. In a large bowl, mix together the scalded milk, sugar, salt, and butter, stirring until the sugar dissolves. Cool to lukewarm.

2. Put the warm water in a large bowl, sprinkle in the yeast, and stir to dissolve. Add the lukewarm milk mixture. Using a wooden spoon, stir in the flour, a little at a time, and then beat vigorously until well blended, about 2 minutes. The batter will be shiny and smooth and leave the sides of the bowl fairly clean. Cover the dough with a clean cloth and let rise in a warm place until slightly more than doubled in volume, about 40 minutes.

3. Preheat the oven to 375°F. Grease a 9 × 5-inch loaf pan.

4. Stir the batter down and beat vigorously for 30 seconds by hand with a wooden spoon. Scoop the batter into the prepared pan.

5. Bake until the loaf is well browned, 40 to 50 minutes. Turn out onto a wire rack to cool.

Peanut Butter MUFFINS

Peanut butter is an ingredient I use for just about anything, even muffins. These are so good and so simple: a moist, cakey, flavorful muffin that's perfect for breakfast or snacktime. Smear the tops with warmed jelly and you have a PB&J.

MAKES 12 MUFFINS

Cooking spray
2 cups all-purpose flour
¼ cup packed light brown sugar
2 tablespoons baking powder
½ teaspoon salt
½ cup creamy peanut butter
1 cup whole milk
1 large egg, lightly beaten
3 tablespoons unsalted butter, melted

1. Preheat the oven to 350°F. Coat 12 cups of a muffin tin with cooking spray.

2. In a food processor, combine the flour, brown sugar, baking powder, and salt. Add the peanut butter and pulse until the mixture resembles coarse crumbs. Add the milk, egg, and melted butter and pulse until combined.

3. Spoon the batter into the prepared muffin cups. Bake until golden brown on top and a toothpick inserted in the center comes out clean, 15 to 20 minutes. Cool in the tin for 20 minutes. Serve warm.

Oatmeal BREAD

I don't really know where this recipe came from; Nana just called it oatmeal bread. After you try it, you're going to call it "Need to Make More" bread. I'm all about good texture when it comes to bread, and this has it. It won't stick to the roof of your mouth like white bread; it's chewy with substance, and there's a hint of sweetness. It's a bread with true grit—in the sense that it sticks to your ribs!

MAKES ONE 8-INCH LOAF

½ cup old-fashioned rolled oats

1½ teaspoons shortening (I use Crisco)

1 cup boiling water

¼ cup warm water (110° to 115°F)

¼ cup molasses

1⅛ teaspoons active dry yeast

2½ cups all-purpose flour, plus more for kneading and shaping the dough

1½ teaspoons salt

1 tablespoon unsalted butter, melted

1. In large bowl, combine the oats and shortening. Pour in the boiling water and let stand until lukewarm.

2. In a small bowl, combine the warm water, molasses, and yeast.

3. In a medium bowl, whisk together the flour and salt. Stir the yeast mixture into the rolled oats and then mix in the flour until combined. Turn out onto a lightly floured surface and knead until smooth, about 5 minutes.

4. Grease a large bowl, add the dough, and brush with the butter. Cover with plastic wrap with a clean kitchen towel over it. Let rise in a warm place until doubled in volume, about 2 hours.

5. Grease an 8 × 5-inch loaf pan. On a lightly floured surface, shape the dough into an 8-inch cylinder. Transfer to the prepared pan, seam-side down, and let rise again until nearly doubled in volume, about 1½ hours.

6. Preheat the oven to 450°F.

7. Bake for 10 minutes. Reduce the oven temperature to 325°F and bake until browned on top, about 1 hour longer.

8. Let cool for 20 minutes in the pan, then unmold and cool slightly on a wire rack. Serve warm. Once cool, the bread can be wrapped tightly in plastic wrap and stored at room temperature for a couple of days.

Banana Nut BREAD

Everyone likes banana bread, but I don't think anyone likes it as much as my husband, Mark, does. I swear he would pick it over a steak. This recipe is a classic, and it's simple to whip up anytime to spoil him. I like white sugar instead of brown because I think you can taste the banana better without the molasses, and I go for butter over oil for the richer flavor.

MAKES ONE 8-INCH LOAF

Cooking spray
2 cups all-purpose flour
1 teaspoon baking soda
½ teaspoon salt
1½ cups sugar
8 tablespoons (1 stick) unsalted butter, at room temperature
2 large eggs
3 really ripe large bananas
1 cup chopped pecans

1. Preheat the oven to 350°F. Coat an 8 × 5-inch loaf pan with cooking spray.

2. In a large bowl, whisk together the flour, baking soda, and salt.

3. Using an electric mixer, beat together the sugar and butter until light and fluffy. Add the eggs, one at a time, and beat again until light and fluffy. Add the bananas, one at a time. Mix in the flour mixture and beat until just combined. Stir in the pecans.

4. Spoon the batter into the prepared loaf pan. Bake until browned and domed on top and a toothpick inserted in the center comes out clean, about 1 hour.

5. Cool for 10 minutes in the pan, then unmold onto a wire rack to cool completely.

Blackberry Pecan BREAD

Wild blackberries are so good that I will fight the briar bushes and snakes in the summertime sun and heat for them. Hopefully I bring home more than I eat, in which case I make this crunchy, sweet bread (which is also good with store-bought berries, mind you). You pair a blackberry with a pecan and I'm in heaven.

MAKES TWO 8-INCH LOAVES

BREAD

Baking spray (with flour)
2 cups all-purpose flour
1 teaspoon baking powder
½ teaspoon baking soda
½ teaspoon ground cinnamon
¼ teaspoon salt
1¼ cups firm fresh blackberries
½ cup chopped pecans
½ cup granulated sugar
½ cup packed light brown sugar
1 large egg
¾ cup whole milk
⅓ cup vegetable oil
2 tablespoons fresh lemon juice
1 teaspoon pure vanilla extract

TOPPING

3 tablespoons granulated sugar
½ teaspoon ground cinnamon

1. Make the bread: Preheat the oven to 350°F. Coat two 8 × 5-inch loaf pans with baking spray.

2. In a large bowl, whisk together the flour, baking powder, baking soda, cinnamon, and salt.

3. In a medium bowl, combine the blackberries and pecans. Add 2 tablespoons of the flour mixture and toss to coat.

4. In a medium bowl, whisk together the granulated sugar, brown sugar, egg, milk, oil, lemon juice, and vanilla. Pour this mixture over the flour mixture and stir with a wooden spoon just until the dry ingredients disappear. Using a rubber spatula, fold in the blackberry

mixture. Divide the batter between the prepared pans.

5. Make the topping: Stir together the granulated sugar and cinnamon and sprinkle over the batter in the pans.

6. Bake until a toothpick inserted in the center comes out clean, 40 to 50 minutes. Let cool in the pans for 10 minutes, then gently unmold onto a wire rack to cool completely.

Peach BREAD

I think it was for the South Carolina Peach Festival one year that I came up with this recipe—but it didn't make it to the festival. When you cook for a competition but don't tell everyone in the house that . . . well, the food doesn't always seem to make it to the competition. But I know it's good enough to disappear when Mama is in the shower. This is the perfect on-the-run, out-the-door breakfast bread, rich in sweet peach flavor and the crunch of nuts. Good hot or cold, all it needs is a little butter.

MAKES ONE 9-INCH LOAF

BREAD
2 cups all-purpose flour
1 teaspoon baking powder
½ teaspoon baking soda
½ teaspoon salt
⅓ cup unsalted butter
¾ cup sugar
2 large eggs
½ teaspoon orange extract
¼ cup buttermilk, peach nectar, or orange juice
1 cup mashed drained canned peaches
½ cup chopped walnuts or pecans

TOPPING
4 tablespoons (½ stick) cold unsalted butter, cut into pieces
1 cup chopped pecans
½ cup packed light brown sugar
1 teaspoon ground cinnamon

1. Make the bread: Preheat the oven to 350°F. Grease and flour a 9 × 5-inch loaf pan.

2. In a large bowl, sift together the flour, baking powder, baking soda, and salt.

3. Using an electric mixer, beat together the butter and sugar until fluffy. Add the eggs, one at a time, beating well after each addition. Beat in the orange extract. Stir in the buttermilk and mashed peaches. Add the flour mixture, mixing just until incorporated. Do not overmix. Using a rubber spatula, fold in the nuts.

4. Pour the batter into the prepared loaf pan.

5. Make the topping: In a bowl, using a fork, combine the butter, pecans, brown sugar, and cinnamon to make a crumbly topping. Sprinkle over the batter in the pan.

6. Bake until browned on top and a toothpick inserted in the center comes out clean, 50 to 60 minutes.

7. Let cool in the pan for 10 minutes before umolding and cooling completely on a wire rack.

Orange Nut LOAF

From my years living in the Sunshine State, I'm still a big fan of anything citrus, including this orange nut bread. In fact, I think this is a recipe I brought back to South Carolina from one of the little church ladies in Florida from my younger years. To mix things up, sometimes I add 3 tablespoons unsweetened cocoa powder with the flour to make orange-chocolate bread.

MAKES ONE 8-INCH LOAF

2 cups all-purpose flour
1 teaspoon baking powder
½ teaspoon baking soda
½ teaspoon salt
2 tablespoons grated orange zest
¾ cup fresh orange juice
2 tablespoons unsalted butter, melted
1 cup sugar
1 large egg, lightly beaten
½ cup chopped walnuts

1. Preheat the oven to 325°F. Grease an 8 × 5-inch loaf pan.

2. In a medium bowl, whisk together the flour, baking powder, baking soda, and salt.

3. In a large bowl, stir together the orange zest, orange juice, melted butter, and sugar. Add the flour mixture and stir with a wooden spoon until smooth.

4. Pour the batter into the prepared loaf pan. Bake until golden and a toothpick inserted in the center comes out clean, about 45 minutes.

5. Cool for 10 minutes in the pan, then unmold onto a wire rack to cool completely.

Acknowledgments

There are so many people I would like to thank . . .

Effie Sahihi, my rock, my role model, who makes me want be a better baker and cook.

Caro Fudo, my Italian stallion and Recap Mason Jar supplier (www.masonjars.com).

Sharon Bowers, my agent, for standing by me in this crazy world of deadlines and I want it yesterdays.

Joe Stallone, my personal Christian Grey and the world's best pit bull attorney.

Sara Remington, one of the best food photographers I have ever met who makes my food mouthwatering.

My girlfriends in The Regal 6, who eat my trial recipes: Deena Spradlin (the adventurous one), Charlie Johnson (the normal one), Sherry Clayton (the caffeinator and Krispy Kreme aficionado), Trudy Dunn (the dependable one), and Carolyn Carruth (the grounded one).

Jamarcus Gatson, my channel 62 producer and foodie eating and moscato wine buddy.

Haygood Mill and Folk Art Center, Pickens, South Carolina.

Ann Volkwein, my kick butt cowriter, who gets my voice and ideas of great food.

Mark Bryson, my husband, for pushing me to always give it my all.

Sarablake Roberts, my daughter, for being my inspiration for making me a better person and mom.

Mama and Daddy, for placing a never-give-up work ethic in me. I hope you both are looking down with smiles; you are missed every day but always on my mind.

All the local bookstores that support a small-town girl who gets to live out her dream.

All of my fans who have stood by me from the beginning of the American Baking Competition.

The amazing folks at Clarkson Potter who stand behind my ideas of true Southern food and make my books possible. Thank you from the bottom of my heart to: **Marysarah Quinn, Stephanie Huntwork, Laura Palese, Sonia Persad, Ian Dingman, Michael Nagin, Cathy Hennessy, Heather Williamson, Lauren Velasquez, Doris Cooper**, and **Aaron Wehner**.

The fabulous **Erica Gelbard Callahan**, a publicity genius, cookie master, and fellow cake-for-breakfast (Kate Spade bag lover) superwoman.

And last but not least my editor, **Rica Allannic**, the one woman in the book world who believed in me enough to give me the chance to do what I always wanted to do and not change who I am with no accent translator.

Index